Herefordshire
MURDERS

NICOLA SLY

The
History
Press

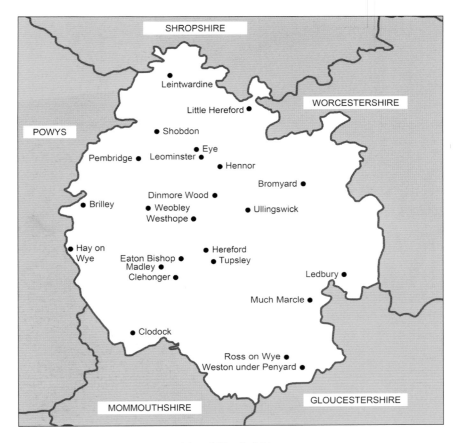

Map of Herefordshire.

First published 2010

The History Press Ltd
The Mill, Brimscombe Port
Stroud, Gloucestershire, GL5 2QG
www.thehistorypress.co.uk

© Nicola Sly, 2010

The right of Nicola Sly to be identified as the Author
of this work has been asserted in accordance with the
Copyrights, Designs and Patents Act 1988.

British Library Cataloguing in Publication Data.
A catalogue record for this book is available from the British Library.

ISBN 978 0 7524 5360 6

Typesetting and origination by The History Press Ltd.
Printed in India, Aegean Offset

CONTENTS

AUTHOR'S NOTE & ACKNOWLEDGEMENTS

Herefordshire is set in the West Midlands of England, bordering Wales to the west. Famed for its charming 'black and white' towns and villages, with their half-timbered buildings, the county is founded on agriculture, especially sheep farming, and the cultivation of apples, pears and hops. Yet historically, beneath the general air of rural tranquility, Herefordshire has a darker side as, like any other county, some of its inhabitants were not averse to taking a human life, whether for love, hate, jealousy, financial gain or simply to rid themself of a person who they perceived as a nuisance.

In 1843, criminal insanity was defined as:

> At the time of the committing of the act, the party accused was labouring under such a defect of reason, from a disease of the mind, as not to know the nature and quality of the act he was doing; or, if he did know it, that he did not know what he was doing was wrong.

This definition would certainly apply to some of the cases included in this collection, such as the murder committed in Brilley in 1848 by Thomas Whitford, who was under the impression at the time that he was battling with the 'great Goddess Diana in the depths of a bottomless pit', or the case of Richard Wreford-Brown, who returned from the First World War a physically and mentally broken man and went on to murder his father-in-law in 1925, while wracked by terrible delusions.

Other featured murders have perhaps more understandable motives, such as the murders of Phillip Ballard in Tupsley in 1887 and Harriet Baker in Ledbury in 1859, both of whom were killed during the course of a robbery. Some murders have a sexual motive, such as that of Ann Dickson in 1885, while others, like the brutal 1935 killing of Edith Nicholls in Shobdon, seem to have absolutely no motive at all. Nicholls' murder remains unsolved, as are others in this collection, among them the 1952 murder of Clehonger shopkeeper, Maria Hill and the killing of Jane Jay in 1878.

The cases were drawn from the archives of local and national newspapers which, along with any books consulted, are listed in the bibliography. Every effort has been made to clear copyright, however my apologies to anyone I may have missed; I can assure you it was not deliberate but an oversight on my part.

As usual, there are a number of people to be thanked for their assistance in compiling this book. I am extremely grateful to the *Hereford Times* for granting permission to use some of their archive pictures as illustrations. The staff at the Hereford Library were very helpful and my brother-in-law and sister-in-law, John and Sue, generously provided accommodation in their home on my research trips to the county.

As always, I must say a special thank you to my husband, Richard, without whose contributions this would be a much poorer volume. Having proof read every word of every chapter, his comments and suggestions proved invaluable. He also acted as chauffeur on my research trips and took several of the photographs.

Last but not least, my grateful thanks go to my editor at The History Press, Matilda Richards, for her continued help and encouragement.

Nicola Sly, 2010

1

'THE FATE OF THIS UNFORTUNATE GIRL NATURALLY EXCITED MUCH COMPASSION'

Clodock, 1790

Twenty-seven-year-old William Jones (aka William Watkins) was a married man with two young children when he first met temptation in the form of an eighteen-year-old prostitute from Monmouth named Suzannah Rugg. Finding himself totally incapable of resisting the nubile teenager's charms, Jones promptly deserted his wife and family and set up home with Suzannah. However, their new-found domestic bliss didn't last long and within weeks he was back living with his wife, Ann, at their home in Clodock.

Their marriage apparently happier than it had ever been, William now treated his wife with unprecedented kindness, even going as far as to prepare meals for her. Yet the errant husband had an ulterior motive and, on 27 March 1790, Ann Jones died in agony, having recently eaten a bowl of broth served to her by William.

With no evident cause of death, surgeons strongly suspected that Ann had been poisoned and performed a post-mortem. William was apparently present throughout the examination, helping to carve open his wife's body without turning a hair and showing neither concern nor surprise when a large quantity of arsenic was found in her stomach.

His nonchalant attitude aroused suspicion and when an inquest jury subsequently arrived at the verdict that Ann Jones had 'died by poison', her husband was arrested on a coroner's warrant and charged with administering the poison that killed his wife. Before long, he was joined in Hereford Gaol by Suzannah Rugg, who was initially charged with the theft of a watch and 6s from a man named Thomas Prosser and then subsequently charged with wilful murder in complicity with her lover, William Jones.

The arsenic found in Ann Jones' stomach was a unique mixture of both the white and the yellow forms of the poison. In the days before the sale of poisons was regulated, arsenic was freely available for over-the-counter purchase and was normally used for killing rats and other vermin. In this case, the combination of white and yellow arsenic was peculiar to one local apothecary, who had accidentally mixed two different consignments of the deadly poison.

Committed for trial at the Hereford Assizes of August 1790, both Jones and Rugg initially appeared confident of acquittal, evidently believing that the evidence against them was purely circumstantial. However, their confidence faded when they were positively identified by the apothecary as the only purchasers of the mixed batch of arsenic.

Both William Jones and Suzannah Rugg were found guilty of the wilful murder of Ann Jones and sentenced to death. Both accepted their fate and made a full confession to the murder, with William Jones taking the opportunity to stress that rumours that he had used the poison to kill any other person were blatantly untrue. The murder of Ann Jones had been premeditated between them – William and Suzannah had intended to marry and had therefore planned to remove the only obstacle that stood in the way of their future happiness. Thus William had initiated a reunion with his wife for the sole purpose of killing her, so that he might legitimately marry the new love of his life.

The now penitent couple were executed at a site opposite the old gaol in Hereford's St Owen Street just two days after the conclusion of their trial. All of the prisoners confined in the gaol at the time were marched outside to witness the execution. Once the two prisoners had met their deaths, a queue of people formed at the scaffold, all anxious to feel the touch of the prisoners' hands on various parts of their bodies, since the touch of a dying criminal's hand was believed at the time to cure warts, boils and cysts and a multitude of other medical conditions.

William Jones was said to have been a dissolute character throughout his life. Before his execution he took steps to ensure that his two children, who would soon be orphaned, were well provided for by signing over property to them and thus guaranteeing them an income of around £40 each year. After his death, his body was removed from the scaffold and hung in chains on the village green at Clodock, close to the place where he had committed his crime, in order to serve as a grim warning to anyone thinking of following in his footsteps.

Suzannah Rugg, who was said to be an exceptionally beautiful young woman, faced her death with a maturity beyond her years, making an impassioned plea from the gallows to the assembled spectators, urging them to be careful of forming unsuitable connections in early life. Her body was handed to surgeons for dissection. According to the *Hereford Journal*:

> The fate of this unfortunate girl naturally excited much compassion:- her wretched mode of life, supposed not to have been adopted or pursued by her own inclination; the influence which Jones may naturally be supposed to have had on her conduct; – her sex – her personal beauty – the unthinkingness of youth – and the frailty of us all – could not fail of being highly interesting in her favour; and though justice might make the sacrifice necessary, humanity may be permitted to shed a tear for the victim!

2

'HE REPEATED THE BLOW SEVERAL TIMES UNTIL I WAS SENSELESS'

Tupsley, 1829

Having once served in the Royal Navy, Francis Wellington of Lugwardine was eligible for a pension from Greenwich Hospital. He was an 'out pensioner', which meant that he didn't actually reside at the hospital but remained living at home with his family and, once every quarter, visited the excise office at Hereford to collect his allowance.

On 3 November 1829, he arrived in Hereford to claim his pension. In anticipation of his quarterly payment, he first called at The Elephant and Castle public house and, from there, went to the excise office where he collected the sum of £5 9s before going back to the pub.

After spending most of the afternoon drinking, by the time Francis Wellington left the pub, various witnesses described him as being 'fresh' and 'forward in beer'. Indeed, he was so drunk that the landlord implored him to stay the night at the pub. Wellington insisted that he was perfectly capable of getting home safely but it quickly became apparent that his confidence was misplaced.

Wellington left the pub at ten o'clock at night and it took him until five o'clock the next morning to walk the four miles between Hereford and his home. He arrived drenched in blood, which had soaked the front of the white smock frock he was wearing and clotted on his face and hands and in his hair. He was missing his hat, gloves, knife and walking stick, not to mention his entire pension.

Wellington's wife, Jane, went upstairs to prepare a bed, leaving the couple's servant, Mrs Baddam, to wash her husband's wounds. However, once the dried blood was removed, Wellington's wounds began to bleed afresh and, having put him to bed with Mrs Baddam's assistance, Jane sent for her husband's doctor.

Francis Wellington suffered from consumption and, even before being injured, was a sickly and exceedingly frail man, whose lungs had deteriorated to such an extent that he persistently coughed up blood and struggled to breathe. When surgeon James Eyre arrived at the Wellingtons' cottage, he found Francis to be 'only partially sensible'. He was apparently in great pain and was running a fever. Eyre examined Wellington and found him to have four wounds on his head, each about three-quarters of an inch long. There was one wound on the right-hand side of his forehead, another on the left-hand side of his head and two more behind his left ear and the surgeon believed that they had all been inflicted by some kind of blunt instrument. He tried to dress the injuries but Wellington struggled and fought so much that Eyre could do very little in the way of treatment.

Eyre called at the cottage again the following morning, finding Wellington still insensible. The surgeon continued to visit regularly over the next few days and his patient's condition gradually improved to the point where he was able to recall the events that led to his injuries, accusing three men of attacking and robbing him as he walked through Tupsley on his way home.

In spite of the return of his memory, Wellington was still a very sick man and Mr Eyre held out little hope for his recovery. Accordingly, on 7 November, Dr Symonds MD – a doctor and local magistrate – was called to his bedside to take his deposition.

Wellington had already named his assailants and stated that one of them was lame and walked with a crutch. The description fitted James Williams, who had been drinking in The Elephant and Castle on the night of the murder, along with two companions, Robert Floyd and John Roberts. The police had been busy scouring the area in search of the culprits and, by 7 November, they had apprehended Floyd, who was brought to Wellington's cottage to hear the deposition. Wellington told the magistrate:

> I received five sovereigns, two half-crowns and four shillings in silver on 3 November at the excise office in Hereford. Going home in Tupsley, I was stopped at about ten o'clock by a lame man with a crutch and another in a blue frock. I defended myself as well as I could till Floyd jumped over the hedge, took my stick from me and knocked me down with a severe blow on the head. He repeated the blow several times until I was senseless. I was robbed of five sovereigns and some silver.

By 10 November, the police had tracked down James Williams and he too was brought to Wellington's bedside in the presence of Dr Symonds. 'Francis [sic] Williams was drinking with me and Floyd in the Elephant and Castle and is the man who first struck me with the crutch,' Wellington now deposed.

The process was repeated on 16 November with the third suspect, John Roberts, in attendance. 'On 3 November I was stopped on the road and violently beaten by two persons in company with Roberts now before me,' stated Wellington.

Wellington's condition continued to deteriorate and he constantly complained of terrible pains in his head, insisting that his bedroom be kept dark at all times since the light hurt his eyes. He also complained of pains in his bowels with accompanying diarrhoea. Eyre called in more doctors for a second opinion and, on 22 December, Wellington was visited at home by Mr John Griffiths and his uncle, also called John Griffiths, both practising as surgeons in Hereford.

Mr Griffiths senior shaved Wellington's head, applying leeches and blistering him, but Wellington showed no signs of improvement. Griffiths visited Wellington several more times and tried a number of different treatments but his patient continued to complain of severe headaches and it was eventually decided to admit him to Hereford Infirmary where he could be under the surgeon's constant care. Thus, on 21 January 1830, Francis Wellington became an in-patient at the hospital and, on admission, was said to be in a much weakened and exhausted state. Nevertheless, he lived until 3 March.

A post-mortem examination was held two days later, attended by all three of the doctors who had been involved in Wellington's care. The surgeons found the scars of the four wounds on Wellington's head, along with a fifth wound that he had received many years earlier while serving in the Navy. Although there were no skull fractures, there was evidence of previous inflammation and ulceration of the *dura mater* – the outermost covering of the brain.

Hereford Infirmary. (Author's collection)

Yet it was the opinion of all three of the doctors that the actual cause of Francis Wellington's death had been lung disease. The dead man's left lung had been completely ravaged by consumption, while the right was covered with suppurating tubercles and was 'full of matter'. John Griffiths junior stated, 'I never saw lungs in a higher state of disease,' and all three doctors expressed surprise that the deceased had managed to live as long as he did, given the appalling degeneration of his lungs and resulting damage to his heart. Not one of the doctors felt able to say with certainty how far Wellington's head injuries had contributed to his demise but Eyre pointed out that, before the night of 3 November, Wellington had never complained of headaches. John Griffiths junior felt that the effect of Wellington's head injuries on his general constitution were such that they would '... tend to wear out life', while his uncle stated,

> The appearances on the brain, I think, arose from the injuries of 3 November and I believe they accelerated death on 3 March by a course of constant irritation, weakening and wearing out the powers of the constitution sooner than they would otherwise have done.

The three men accused of attacking and robbing him now found themselves charged in connection with his death and were brought to trial at the Hereford Assizes on 31 March 1830, before Mr Baron Bolland. Thirty-five-year-old Robert Floyd was charged with wilful murder, while James Williams, aged nineteen, and seventeen-year-old John Roberts, were charged with aiding and abetting him.

Having outlined the events of 3 November 1829, counsel for the prosecution, Mr Serjeant Russell, told the members of the jury that they had three questions to answer; had Wellington been beaten and robbed as he had stated, did the violent treatment he received cause or even hasten his death and, if the jury answered yes to the first two questions, were the defendants the persons who inflicted those injuries? Russell advised the jury that, in a previous case, Lord Hale had laid down a ruling that '...if a man be sick of a disease that might end him in half a year and another strikes him a blow which hastens his death by the irritation and provocation of that disease then the offence is murder.'

The prosecution counsel told the court that all three of the defendants had been present at The Elephant and Castle pub on the evening of 3 November and that Floyd, who was a Chelsea out-pensioner, had even been present at the excise office when Wellington received his pension. During the course of the evening's drinking, Wellington had pulled a coin from his pocket to pay for his beer. In the dimly lit bar, he had mistakenly proffered a sovereign rather than the intended shilling. Later in the evening, he dropped several coins on the floor, which James Williams picked up and returned to him, advising him to put his money safely in his pocket. Instead, Wellington placed the coins on the table, in full view of all of the other drinkers at the pub.

The court next heard from the medical witnesses, who all stated that Wellington's death was ultimately due to consumption. However, all had noticed some yellow patches on Wellington's brain at the post-mortem examination, beneath which the brain appeared softened and spongy, along with some inflammation at the front of the brain beneath the site of the wound on his forehead. None of the doctors were able to state conclusively that the injuries to his head and brain had killed him but all conceded that the wounds would have caused him more stress, pain and discomfort, which his disease-ravaged body just could not tolerate. All of the doctors were of the opinion that the head wounds had thus accelerated Wellington's death although he was so ill that, even had he not been injured, his life expectancy would have been very short. Mr Griffiths senior went as far as to say that, disregarding Wellington's existing lung disease, the damage to his brain following the attack on him was sufficiently severe to eventually cause his death.

Once the medical witnesses had testified, the judge consulted with the jury, asking if, having heard the medical evidence, they felt the case should proceed. He reminded them that none of the surgeons could positively state that the damage to Wellington's brain had been caused by the attack on him and that the observed changes to the brain could have resulted from his advanced lung disease or from the damage it had caused to his heart.

After a short consultation, the jury decided that it was pointless to continue trying the defendants for murder or for aiding and abetting a murder, since they could not be absolutely sure that a murder had even been committed. The judge dismissed the case and immediately began a second trial in which all three of the defendants were charged with assault and highway robbery.

As a result of testimony from James Jones, the clerk to the collector of excise at Hereford, it was established that Wellington had received his pension on 3 November, as had the defendant Robert Floyd.

The landlord of The Elephant and Castle told the court that Wellington and the three defendants had all been drinking in his establishment on the afternoon of the murder. Floyd had left first at about half-past nine in the evening, followed about half an hour later by Francis Wellington, who was drunk at the time although still capable of walking, albeit with a slight stagger. Within minutes of Wellington's departure, Roberts had gone outside for about five minutes, returning and saying to Williams 'He is gone'. At that, both Williams and Roberts drained their drinks and quickly left the pub.

The landlord's evidence was corroborated by his son and by some of the other customers who had been drinking in the pub that night. Without exception, all of the witnesses stated that Wellington had been wearing a clean, white smock. His stick, gloves, handkerchief, knife and hat had been returned to his widow after his death, having been found on the side of the road by a Mr Field and handed to Jonathon Baddam, the husband of the Wellingtons' servant, who immediately realised to whom they belonged. Field and Baddam told the court that there had been a great deal of blood on the ground nearby. Unfortunately, the handkerchief and stick had been heavily bloodstained and Jane Wellington had subsequently burned them.

The court next heard details of Wellington's various depositions, followed by the evidence of the arrests of the suspects by Mr Howell, the City Constable of Hereford, after which the prosecution closed.

The counsel for Floyd's defence, Mr Curwood, then took the floor and introduced witnesses who stated that his client had been nowhere near the scene of the murder. Mary Huggins insisted that Floyd had spent the night with her at the home of Elizabeth Wilcox, also known as Elizabeth England. Mary remembered that it had been pension day and that, when Floyd first arrived, she had clearly seen the church clock, which stood at a quarter to nine. Elizabeth Wilcox and another woman, Elizabeth Pearce, backed up her evidence as did many other witnesses.

There was a large, gaping crack in the wall of Elizabeth Wilcox's home that was approximately 3ft wide and 4ft high. Several people insisted that they had either seen or heard Robert Floyd through the hole in the wall on the night of the murder.

Mr Baron Bolland then summarised the evidence for the jury, placing particular emphasis on the alleged drunkenness of the victim on leaving The Elephant and Castle. Francis Wellington was a frail, sick man and the amount of alcohol he had consumed would have affected even a man in perfect health. The jury must ask themselves whether Wellington was capable of identifying the three men who had attacked him on a dark night. It must be recalled that he had struggled to tell the difference between a sovereign and a shilling earlier on the night of his death but that he had been able to see sufficiently well to rectify his mistake. While the victim's depositions were an important part of the evidence, the three prisoners who had witnessed them had not asked Wellington any questions at the time and it was not absolutely certain that they had been advised that they were allowed to do so. With the charge of murder against them dismissed, the prisoners stood accused of assault and, under normal circumstances, their victim would be in court to tell his story and submit to cross-examination.

The inaccuracy of one point had already been established, since Wellington had deposed that he was set upon at about ten o'clock in the evening. Witnesses had stated that he was still in the pub at that time, a distance of a mile and a half from where he was attacked. The judge also pointed out some inconsistencies in the statements made by those who had testified to Robert Floyd's presence in Mrs Wilcox's home at the time of the murder, which were contradictory to the statements of the witnesses in the pub. Those who placed Floyd with Mary Huggins swore that he was there from 8.45 p.m., while the landlord and customers in the pub had all stated that he had not left until 9.30 p.m. There had been some suggestion in court that one witness, John Taylor, had spoken to Mr Howell to try and find out the exact time of the attack, with the express purpose of providing an alibi for Floyd, something which Taylor strongly denied.

'I, for my own part, approach the evidence with fear and trembling,' concluded the judge, calling on the jury to apply their judgement only to the evidence they had heard in court that day, expunging from their minds all previous information and every former impression they may have held about the case.

The jury needed only a few minutes of deliberation to pronounce all three defendants 'Guilty' of the charges against them. The judge deferred sentencing to the following day, when he meted out the death penalty to all three of the accused.

As John Roberts was only seventeen years old and had apparently taken no active part in the attack on Francis Wellington, his death sentence was later commuted to one of transportation for life. Meanwhile, as the date set for the execution of Floyd and Williams approached, there were grave doubts about Robert Floyd's involvement and he was given a stay of execution until 15 May while further investigations were made. Williams seemed truly repentant and acknowledged the justice of his sentence but, regardless of their own punishment, both he and Roberts swore that Floyd had taken no part in the attack.

Thus it was only James Williams who mounted the scaffold at Hereford Gaol on 17 April 1830, where he was executed for the crime of highway robbery. Although the eventual outcome was the same, it was widely argued at the time that, having deprived a man of his last remaining time on earth, according to Lord Hale's ruling, his actions on the night of 3 November amounted to nothing less than murder.

3

'YOU HAVE ROBBED ME — FOR GRACIOUS SAKE, DON'T MURDER ME'

Hereford, 1831

Whenever the Assizes came to town there was money to be made and thirty-six-year-old Mrs Susan Connop was always keen to make money. Susan kept a brothel in Worcester but on 22 March 1831, two days before the Lent Assizes were due to commence at Hereford, she and some of her best girls took up residence there at the home of Joseph Pugh in Quaker Lane.

Sixty-year-old Walter Carwardine had more legitimate business at the Assizes, in the form of a lawsuit with one of his brothers. However, once the case had been heard, Carwardine's thoughts quickly turned from business to pleasure.

The farmer from Kinnersley was known to be a heavy drinker, with an equal fondness for food, so his first priority was a visit to the local hostelries. He dined at the Horse & Groom public house in Eign Street, leaving there at around eight o'clock in the evening and moving to the Red Streak, a pub he had already visited that morning. At the Horse & Groom, he was seen by his brother, William, who noted that he '...appeared to have taken too much liquor.'

With his appetites for food and drink satisfied, Carwardine turned his attention to his appetite for women. He was 'picked up' by Susan Reignart, one of Susan Connop's girls, who took him back to Joseph Pugh's house, where he sat on an armchair drinking gin, with Reignart on his knee.

The Horse & Groom, Eign Street, Hereford, 2009. (© R. Sly)

Soon afterwards, another prostitute, Sarah Coleby, decided that she wanted to take care of Mr Carwardine, so she and Reignart exchanged clients, with Susan taking butcher John Webb upstairs to one of the bedrooms. When she eventually came downstairs again, it was to see Sarah secretively showing something to Mrs Connop, who winked and indicated to her that she should put it in her pocket. Susan Connop then asked Susan Reignart if she thought Carwardine had any money. 'I'll have his money or his life,' she vowed. 'If I can't manage in any other way, I'll have him put in a bag.'

Carwardine gave Mrs Connop a shilling to fetch yet more gin but before she could return, he announced his intention of going to look for somewhere to sleep. Sarah Coleby offered to go with him and she and the farmer left the house together. When Susan Connop came back, she asked where Carwardine had gone and, when Susan Reignart couldn't tell her, she asked her if she thought that Sarah had robbed him. Mrs Connop then went out to look for Sarah, returning to the house with her a few minutes later. Almost as soon as they had come back, William Williams and John Mathews burst into the house, slamming the door shut behind them.

Seconds later, there was a loud knocking on the door, accompanied by Carwardine's voice shouting, 'Open the door, for I am robbed'. Mrs Connop sent Williams to answer the door, telling him to make Carwardine say that he hadn't been robbed on her premises, which he did. Joseph Pugh also went to try and get the farmer to leave his doorstep, saying, 'Damn your eyes, if you don't be off, I'll send you.' Meanwhile, Sarah Coleby had snatched up her bonnet and shawl and fled out of the back door, while Williams and Mathews went outside to speak to Carwardine.

Susan Reignart went to bed alone at around midnight and was rudely awakened about an hour later by a series of fearsome crashes and bangs from downstairs. Curious, she got out of bed and crept along the landing to see what was going on.

Mrs Connop shouted up the stairs, 'Susan, do not get up yet.' 'Very well,' replied Susan, although she remained on the landing, listening intently to the commotion from below. Suddenly, she heard a crash so loud that it actually shook the staircase, followed by the sound of the front door and the outside gate slamming and Mrs Connop's voice saying, 'We have done it.'

Walter Carwardine never arrived home to Kinnersley and two or three days later his hat was found at Monk's Hole, on the banks of the River Wye. William Carwardine had already been to Hereford to search for his missing brother, finding no trace of him. Now William received an unsolicited visit from a man who introduced himself as Mr Pearce, saying that he owned three barges and was prepared to search the river for Walter Carwardine's body. He assured William that the search would not be too expensive.

William told Pearce that he had already checked the river and not found his brother and that he believed that Walter would make his way home eventually. Pearce however was insistent, telling William that he knew exactly where the body was because a hat had been found. Still William refused to take Pearce up on his offer. Soon afterwards, the news reached William that his brother's body had been found in the river by a boatman, about two miles outside Hereford. Pearce then approached him again and told William that it had been he who had found his brother's hat, asking him for some form of reward for doing so.

Having no knowledge of his brother's movements after leaving the Horse & Groom and being aware that Walter had then been very drunk, William assumed that his brother had accidentally stumbled into the river on his way home and drowned. However, a post-mortem examination of Walter's body seemed to indicate otherwise, as several wounds were found on his head. Doctors were unable to state with any certainty that any of these injuries would ultimately have proved fatal, but were of the opinion that Carwardine had been thrown into the water when he was either dead or unconscious. His body exhibited none of the characteristic marks of a person who had died from drowning and, since his head wounds were both bruised and swollen, it was thought that they had been inflicted while he was alive. The doctors were unable to pinpoint the precise cause of Walter Carwardine's death, although they unanimously opined that it was due to suffocation rather than drowning.

An investigation began into the suspicious death of Walter Carwardine and before long Susan Connop found herself with yet more business at the Hereford Assizes. This time, there was no money to be made, since she was arrested at

Worcester and charged with Carwardine's wilful murder, with Joseph Pugh also charged as an accessory after the fact.

Their trial opened before Mr Justice Patteson on 6 August. Mr Curwood, for the prosecution, told the court that the victim had not been seen alive since the night of 24 March 1831. Curwood first called Carwardine's sister, Mary, who stated that when her brother left home to go to the Assizes, he was carrying a £5 note issued by the Kington bank. Mary admitted that Walter was '...rather addicted to drinking'.

John Webb, who had been availing himself of the services offered by Mrs Connop's girls on the night in question, told the court that Carwardine had been at Joseph Pugh's house and that he had twice called for gin to be sent for. Webb left the house at between eleven o'clock and midnight, at which time Carwardine was alive and well, if very drunk.

Mr Curwood next called Mary Bachelor, who lived directly opposite Pugh's house. Mrs Bachelor had particular reason to remember the night of 24/25 March, since she had passed it watching the corpse of her child. She stated that, at about a quarter to one on the morning of 25 March, she heard a noise coming from Pugh's house and had opened her window to see what was happening. A stout man had been at Pugh's door shouting that he had been robbed. Mary then saw Susan Connop come to the door and strike the man on the back of his neck with either a short stick or a poker, at which he had begged, 'Have mercy on me! You have robbed me – for gracious sake, don't murder me.'

The man attempted to run away but Susan Connop followed him, all the while beating him about the head. There were two other men present and they too began to belabour the man with their fists, while Susan ran back to the house and shouted for everybody to leave. Emanuel Horwell, who lived about 20 yards from Pugh's house, was also disturbed by the fracas and corroborated Mary Bachelor's evidence.

Mary Ann Williams, one of Mrs Connop's girls, told the court that she had left Pugh's house at midnight and gone to walk about the town, looking for 'business'. On her return at around one o'clock, she saw Carwardine leaning against the wall of the premises of a coach maker, Mr Thomas. Her sighting was corroborated by Edward Lewis, who knew Carwardine well.

Susan Reignart testified to picking up Carwardine in Hereford and taking him back to Pugh's house. She related the events of the evening, ending with her account of going to bed alone and being woken up by the sounds of a fight downstairs. Once things had quietened down, she recalled Joseph Pugh emerging rather drunk from another upstairs room and asking Mrs Connop, 'Have you robbed the man?'

Susan Connop insisted that she hadn't but Joseph insisted, 'I am afraid you have and murdered him too,' at which Mrs Connop and Sarah Coleby began to cry. Susan Reignart had then gone back to bed and, on the following day, Mrs Connop had taken her girls back to Worcester. However on the journey home,

Sarah Coleby had pulled a Kington bank £5 note from the bindings of her bonnet and she also had a great deal of silver coinage about her person. Reignart finally said that on the day Susan Connop and her girls were arrested, Connop had said to her, 'Let us both be in the same tale.'

As soon as Susan Reignart had finished her testimony, Mr Justice Patteson dramatically halted the case, saying that he feared there was insufficient evidence to sustain the present charges, even though the circumstances of the case were of very great suspicion. With that, the defendants were both acquitted.

Yet this wasn't to be Susan Connop's last visit to the Hereford Assizes since in March 1832, she appeared as a principal witness in the trial of Joseph Pugh, William Williams and John Mathews, who had now been jointly charged with Carwardine's murder. Coincidentally, their trial before Mr Justice Taunton opened on 24 March – the first anniversary of Carwardine's death.

The case was prosecuted by Mr C. Phillips, assisted by the appropriately named Mr Justice. Phillips first called witnesses from the Horse & Groom and the Red Streak public houses, who informed the court that Walter Carwardine had been drinking there on the night of 24 March. This was confirmed by William Carwardine, who had seen his brother in the Horse & Groom and had next seen his body on the banks of the Wye on 12 April 1831.

John Webb was again brought before the court to testify to having been in Pugh's house and the prosecution then called several witnesses who lived nearby and had seen various occurrences in the vicinity.

Mary Lerigo, a single woman who lived just up the street, had heard a man on Pugh's doorstep bemoaning the fact that he had been robbed. Soon afterwards, she heard a scuffle and, on opening her door to investigate, saw a fight going on in the street. Mathews and Williams were present, as was a local shoemaker named George Corner and a watchman. Mary had also seen a person she described as 'a lusty man' walking along Quaker Lane, apparently searching for a particular house.

George Corner had also seen 'the lusty man' in the company of Mathews and Williams. Corner had been on his way to visit his father with his brother when he happened upon the three men in Quaker Lane. Mathews asked him what his business was and Corner replied, 'The road is as free to me as it is to you.' At that, Mathews punched him, knocking him against a door, while Williams challenged Corner's brother to fight, which he declined to do. Corner's father, Richard, came out of his house to find out what was happening and was also punched for his trouble.

Mary Bachelor repeated her testimony from the previous trial, adding that she was absolutely certain about her identification of 'the lusty man' as the victim since, when Susan Connop had come to the door, she was carrying a candle, which illuminated the scene sufficiently for Bachelor to be able to see his clothing, now produced as evidence in court.

The next witness to be called was prostitute Mary Ann Williams. Twenty-year-old Williams told the court that she had been 'an unfortunate girl' for about four or five years. Shortly after the trial of Susan Connop and Joseph Pugh, Mary Ann was badly beaten by Pugh and William Williams' brother. Fearing that she was dying from her injuries, she went to Mr Howell, the sword bearer and City Constable of Hereford and, before Howell and Hereford Mayor John Farmer, made a voluntary statement.

Mary Ann admitted that she had not told the truth at the previous trial, saying that she had been too frightened to do so. In her statement dictated on 23 August 1831, which she made under the impression that she did not have long to live, she said that she had left Pugh's with Mr Webb the butcher, walking with him as far as the King's Head Inn in Broad Street before returning to the house. On her return journey, she passed the premises of coach maker Mr Thomas, where she saw Mathews, Williams, Pugh and Sarah Coleby with Walter Carwardine. She clearly heard Carwardine saying, 'For God's sake, don't murder me,' and stated that Sarah had told the men, 'I have got his "blunt" and if you will keep secret, I will treat.'

Williams said, 'I will soon put him out of the way,' and had then struck Carwardine, who fell to the ground, groaning as if he were dying. His groans were the last sound Mary Ann heard as Williams spotted her and pulled her away. Standing in Quaker Lane, Mary Ann said she distinctly heard the voices of Pugh, Williams, Mathews and Coleby cursing Carwardine and, frightened, had returned to Pugh's house and gone to bed.

Mary Ann swore that she was now telling the truth. She had voluntarily made her statement to the Mayor not out of a wish for revenge for the terrible beating she had received but because she believed that she was dying and wanted to clear her conscience and make herself 'fit to die'. She informed the court that she was no longer working as a prostitute but was now living in Ross-on-Wye, under the protection of a man, supporting herself as a needlewoman.

Susan Connop was the next witness to appear and she now corroborated Mary Ann's deposition, as did Elizabeth Powell and her husband, who had both seen the fight with Carwardine and witnessed Williams propelling an obviously frightened Mary Ann away from the scene, his arm around her waist.

The prosecution then dealt with the finding of Walter Carwardine's body, first calling Thomas Pearce, who had found his hat on the riverbank. They then recalled William Carwardine, who testified to receiving a visit from Mr Pearce, offering to search for his brother's body. However, the 'Mr Pearce' who approached William Carwardine was not Thomas Pearce but William Williams. On hearing this evidence, Williams immediately denied ever having approached Carwardine, even though Carwardine positively identified him in court.

Solicitor Mr Watkyns had watched Carwardine's body being removed from the river and recalled William Williams being present at the time and helping to move the body. Watkyns had seen the wounds on the dead man's head, which Williams had promptly covered with a handkerchief. At the time, Watkyns believed that he had done this as a matter of common decency but now he thought that the covering of Carwardine's face had been an attempt by Williams at concealment of his injuries.

After hearing medical evidence about these injuries, the prosecution's final witness was William Howell, the sword bearer of Hereford, who stated that Mary Ann Williams had made her statement voluntarily and that a subsequent statement had been made by a girl named Sarah Powell – presumably the daughter of witnesses Elizabeth Powell and her husband – which had exactly matched Mary Ann's account. With that, the prosecution rested.

The judge then called upon each of the three prisoners to speak in his own defence. Joseph Pugh simply stated that he had been in bed with Susan Reignart all night and had not left the house.

William Williams denied ever having approached William Carwardine and pretending that his name was Pearce. He admitted to assisting with the removal of the body from the river, asking the court if it was likely that he would have done so if he had murdered the deceased. He insisted that he would have been more likely to use the time before the body was found to make good an escape, had he been Carwardine's murderer.

Finally, John Mathews told the court that, on hearing the charge against him, he had voluntarily gone to Mayor John Farmer to try and sort things out. He too insisted that, had he been involved in Carwardine's death, he would have fled the area rather than handing himself over to the authorities.

Susan Reignart was recalled and said that Pugh had not slept with her all night as he had stated but had been asleep in a different bedroom. Although she wasn't aware of him leaving the house at any time, he could easily have done so without her noticing.

Richard Corner was called to give his recollections of the fight between his sons and Williams and Mathews in an attempt to demonstrate that, having gone to investigate on hearing the noise of the fight outside his home, he would surely have heard any subsequent fight between the defendants and Carwardine.

Witnesses provided Williams and Mathews with alibis for the time of the attack, although these proved somewhat unsatisfactory since these witnesses were either related to the defendants or were associated with living in or keeping a brothel and their evidence contradicted that given by every other witness who had already testified.

Finally, character witnesses were called, although only Mathews could muster somebody who was prepared to speak on his behalf. Mathews originated from Brecon and was the son of a highly respected tradesman. Several witnesses, including Revd Morgan Price of Brecon, gave him an excellent character witness, many stating that he was only in his present predicament because of his association with William Williams. Williams was described as a fine-looking young man, although of desperate character. One of his brothers had been hanged and he had another brother and a sister who had been transported. A third brother was currently in prison for deserting from the Army.

According to the contemporary newspaper reports of the trial, Williams remained cool and almost indifferent to his surroundings, until Mary Ann Williams was called to the witness box. He gave her an imploring look that forced her to turn her head aside to avoid his gaze. His face had alternately flushed and paled, his lips trembled and his breathing became a series of shallow gasps, illustrating his internal agitation.

Pugh had also been affected by the evidence against him. Described as 'an ill-looking fellow of very bad character', at the start of the proceedings he behaved with 'disgusting levity', laughing and clowning about to the extent that his own counsel had been forced to rebuke him. However, as the trial progressed, his confidence had deserted him, replaced by terror and dismay, and his face had shown 'intense mental agony'.

After a trial lasting almost twelve hours, the judge summed up the evidence and the jury retired for fifteen minutes, returning to pronounce all three defendants 'Guilty' of the charges against them. All three men appeared surprised at the verdict. The judge ordered them to be hanged in two days time, their bodies afterwards given to the surgeons for dissection.

Thus twenty-seven-year-old Joseph Pugh, twenty-four-year-old William Williams and twenty-five-year-old John Mathews were executed at a triple hanging at Hereford Gaol on 26 March 1832. All three protested their innocence to their last breaths.

Note: There are some variations in spelling in the contemporary newspaper accounts of the murder. Defendant John Mathews is also called Matthews, witness Mary Bachelor is also referred to as Batchelor, while Sarah Coleby is also named Sarah Coltby and Sarah Coley. The sword bearer of Hereford is named both as Mr Howell and Mr Howells.

4

'LUCY, LUCY — WHY DO YOU NOT SPEAK TO ME?'

Westhope, 1842

Thomas Parker died in February 1842, leaving the four properties that he owned on his death to his wife, Lucy. Yet, while Lucy might be a wealthy widow, there was a frisson of gossip around the village of Westhope that she might not have been an entirely faithful wife. Thomas Parker had been particularly suspicious of one young man, William Powell, and soon after Parker's death, Powell and his seventy-two-year-old mother, Mary, moved in with Lucy. By May, the village gossip had reached a new intensity when it was announced that William and Lucy were to be married.

At twenty-seven, William was almost twenty-one years younger than his prospective bride and even more scandalous was the fact that Lucy Parker was the blood sister of Mary Powell, making her William's aunt. In 1506, the Church of England drew up a list of forbidden marriages, '... wherein whosoever are related are forbidden in scripture and our laws to marry together'. The list, which remains largely unchanged today, clearly showed that a marriage between aunt and nephew was not permitted. In spite of this, the banns for William and Lucy's marriage had been read at the local church twice and would be read for the third and final time on 29 May 1842. Although there was universal disapproval of the marriage in the village, it seemed that nobody was prepared to speak out and call a halt to the proceedings.

On 28 May, James Bounds had cause to walk by Lucy Parker's house several times during the course of the day and, at eight o'clock at night, he saw William

Westhope. (© N. Sly)

Powell standing by the window, holding a letter in his hand. Powell seemed extremely angry at something and Bounds heard him shouting, 'Why did you keep it from me?'

Mary Powell then shouted back at her son, 'Her didn't keep it from you. Her knew nothing about it,' but William was not to be placated.

'You are a whore and I will kill you and break everything in the house,' he raged, addressing somebody unseen by Bounds. The crash of breaking glass and a loud thumping noise coming from within the house suggested that William was putting his threats into immediate action. There followed the sounds of a brief scuffle and, seconds later, Lucy Parker appeared at the door shouting 'Murder!' She repeated her cry several times before Bounds saw William Powell appear behind her and drag her back into the house, after which everything went quiet.

Unfortunately for Lucy, there had been all too frequent violent arguments between her and her future husband and mother-in-law since their cohabitation and Bounds thought that this was just the latest of them. Since it appeared from the silence that peace had been restored, he continued on his way without intervening.

Thirty minutes later, James Colley went to Lucy Parker's house to pay her some money that he owed her. When he rang the bell, Mary answered the door and told him that Lucy was not at home. Just as Colley was about to leave, William shouted from indoors, 'Is that you, James? Come in.'

Colley walked into the house to find Lucy sitting in an armchair, apparently unconscious. William was bending over her, dabbing at her face with a wet handkerchief and, when Colley asked him what had happened, William replied airily, 'Oh, nothing. Only a bit of an accident.'

It was obvious to Colley that, whatever had occurred at Lucy's house, it was far more serious than 'a bit of an accident'. Lucy was bleeding heavily from her chin and neck and had a mark on her throat that looked to have been made by a man's hand. The floor was wet, as if it had very recently been washed and there were spots of blood on the walls and windows, as well as on the front of William's shirt and waistcoat.

Colley went to fetch the nextdoor neighbour, Mary Anne Warwick, who arrived to find William holding a mirror in front of Lucy to try and determine whether or not she was breathing. The mirror appeared slightly misted and, to Mary Anne, William seemed distraught. 'Lucy, Lucy – why do you not speak to me?' he repeatedly asked the senseless woman.

While William continued to try and revive Lucy, Mary Anne asked Mary what had happened and was told that Lucy had met with an accident and fallen down. When it finally became obvious to William that his efforts were proving unsuccessful, he went upstairs and put on a clean shirt and his best suit. He then asked Mary Anne to stay with his mother while he walked the four miles to Leominster to inform attorney and magistrate Mr Lloyd of what had happened.

When William related his sorry story in the presence of parish constable, Thomas Munn, Munn formed the impression that he was under the influence of alcohol. He arrested Powell and escorted him back to the house and, by the time they arrived, a surgeon had pronounced Lucy Parker dead and her body had been moved upstairs to her bedroom. William asked if he might see her again before being taken away to Hereford Gaol. Permission was granted and, for several minutes, William stood before Lucy's body without speaking, silent tears rolling down his face. Mary Powell was also arrested as, although she insisted that Lucy had simply fallen over, her own body bore the marks of a recent violent altercation.

A post-mortem examination, conducted by surgeons Mr Watling and Mr Meredith, found evidence of numerous blows to Lucy's head, which they believed had been made with a blunt instrument. There were several round bruises, consistent in size and shape with the head of a large carpenter's hammer found on a table in the scullery. Both of the surgeons also believed that a considerable amount of pressure had been applied to Lucy's throat, probably to prevent her from crying out. In the opinion of both doctors, the combination of the blows to the deceased's head, which had caused bleeding in her brain, coupled with pressure on her windpipe, had caused Lucy's death and she could not possibly have died following an accidental fall.

Mr Watling was also called to examine William and Mary Powell at Leominster police station and found that Mary too was badly bruised. There was a bruise on the left side of her face, beneath her lower jaw and a massive bruise measuring nine inches by four inches on her left arm. One of her fingers was cut and there was a further bruise on one collarbone. However, no bruises or other marks of violence were found on William.

At the inquest into the death of Lucy Parker, the coroner's jury returned a verdict of manslaughter against William and Mary Powell. However, magistrates subsequently decided that a charge of wilful murder was more appropriate for William and he was committed to stand trial at the next Hereford Assizes.

The trial opened on 2 August 1842, with Mr Justice Erskine presiding. William Powell was charged with the wilful murder of Lucy Parker, while Mary was charged with murder in the second degree, having aided and abetted her son in the commission of the murder. Both defendants were also indicted on the coroner's warrant on charges of manslaughter. They were defended by Mr W.H. Cooke, who was up against Mr Greaves for the prosecution.

It emerged that the letter seen in William's hand by James Bounds, which had so angered him, came from an unimaginatively named villager, George George, who had written to Lucy offering to marry her and suggesting a clandestine meeting between them to discuss the matter further. In spite of his mother's insistence that 'Her knew nothing about it', on reading the letter, William had instantly assumed that Lucy had been carrying on an intimate relationship with George behind his back and had flown into a rage.

The prosecution maintained that a violent fracas had ensued, during which William and Mary had together beaten Lucy Parker to death. Counsel for the defence, Mr Cooke, disagreed and put up a spirited argument on behalf of both of his clients.

The only evidence against Mary Powell was her assertion that her sister died as a result of a fall, coupled with the fact that Mary herself was covered in bruises that appeared to indicate that she had recently been engaged in a fight. It was only natural for Mary to wish to shield her son from the awful consequences of a murder trial. Yet her words, 'Her didn't keep it from you. Her knew nothing about it', clearly heard by James Bounds, seemed to indicate that she was trying to defend her sister by defusing her son's anger. It was thus highly possible that Mary's bruises had occurred as a result of trying to protect her sister against William and, if they believed that this was the case, then the jury should acquit her of all charges against her.

Cooke then dealt with the case against William Powell, asking if it was likely that he would have murdered his bride-to-be only a few days before their wedding, after which he would have become her rightful heir and entitled to inherit her considerable wealth. The letter sent by George George, with the sole purpose of transferring Lucy's affections from William to himself, was sufficient to excite William's feelings and provoke his anger, particularly if he was of the opinion that he had been cuckolded on the verge of his marriage.

Cooke then went on to challenge the medical evidence, asking if it was likely that heavy blows from a hammer could have bruised the victim's head without breaking her skin. Reminding the jury that James Bounds had already testified to seeing William dragging Lucy back into the house, he asked whether or not the apparent pressure to her windpipe might have occurred then.

Throughout his defence counsel's entire speech, William Powell wept bitterly, burying his face in his handkerchief and sometimes leaning forward so that his forehead rested on the rail at the front of the dock. His sobs continued as Mr Justice Erskine commenced his summary of the evidence for the jurors, which was to last for almost two hours.

Erskine advised the jury that they must first satisfy themselves that the death of Lucy Parker was occasioned by acts of violence towards her head. If they were so satisfied, he told them, then it was not necessary to consider the actual implement used to inflict those blows, whether it was the hammer produced in court or not – what they should be considering was whether or not the violence was caused by any act of the male prisoner. If the blows were occasioned by the male prisoner, were they justified by any acts of the deceased because, had he been attacked and acted in self-defence, the prisoner would not be responsible for the crime of murder but manslaughter? Erskine then reminded the jury that no evidence had been produced to show that Lucy Parker had in any way provoked the violence against her and that the law demanded that any violence against her must be deemed malicious unless the contrary was shown. He reiterated that, on examination after his arrest, there had been absolutely no marks of violence seen on William Powell, which would indicate that Lucy had not struck him.

The jury retired only briefly before returning to court with their verdicts. Mary Powell was acquitted of all charges against her, while William was found 'Not Guilty' of wilful murder but 'Guilty' of the manslaughter of Lucy Parker. He was promptly sentenced to transportation for life.

Note: Witness James Bounds is alternatively named James Bownes in some contemporary accounts of the murder.

5

'YOU HAVE BROUGHT ME INTO A FINE SCRAPE'

Much Marcle, 1842

In 1842, the gossip circulating around the village of Much Marcle was that thirty-year-old Milborough Trilloe was pregnant and that the father of her unborn child was a gentleman from Ross-on-Wye. Milborough – a widow who already had three children – vehemently denied any pregnancy, telling her landlord James Taylor that people could talk all they wanted but the rumours simply weren't true. Yet inevitably time proved otherwise and, as her belly swelled, she was eventually forced to admit that she was with child. Taylor, a widower, was in the habit of making regular visits to his tenant and sometimes called on her as often as ten times a day. The frequency of his appearances at the cottage led some villagers to speculate that he was the father of Milborough's unborn child, something which he always denied.

Milborough and her children shared the house with another woman, Sarah Scrivens, who, although unmarried, had herself given birth to six children, four of whom had either been stillborn or had died shortly after birth. When Milborough could no longer deny her pregnancy, Sarah questioned her about the fact that she seemed to be making no preparations for the child's birth. Milborough assured Sarah that her baby would not survive since it was 'too restless' inside her. Sarah argued that a restless baby was more likely to live than one that didn't move as much but Milborough was adamant that her child wouldn't live, saying that, in the unlikely event that it did, she had an old dress that she could wrap it in.

On 24 June 1842, Milborough woke in the morning and complained of feeling very cold, which Sarah took as a sign that she was nearing her confinement. Both

Much Marcle. (© N. Sly)

women normally worked as farm labourers, earning sixpence a day for hoeing weeds and Milborough also supplemented her income by doing washing and mending for their landlord. When Sarah went out to work at between five and six o'clock that morning, she left Milborough shivering miserably in bed.

After a long day at work in the fields, Sarah returned home at about eight o'clock that evening to find Milborough still in bed. Sarah asked her if she had got up at all that day and Milborough replied that she hadn't. As Milborough was dressed only in her chemise, Sarah couldn't help but notice that she was no longer pregnant. When Sarah questioned her, Milborough told her that she had suffered a miscarriage and that James Taylor had already buried the dead baby.

Having given birth and knowing the great pain involved in doing so, Sarah asked if she had requested the services of Mrs Baldwin, the midwife, to assist her in delivering the child. Milborough said that she had sent for Mrs Baldwin but she had refused to come, telling her that the child wouldn't live anyway. Milborough insisted that, had she known that she was about to give birth, she would have paid Sarah sixpence to stay home from work and assist her.

It had been quite an eventful day in the household since, as well as Milborough's miscarriage, Sarah's young daughter had badly burned her arm. Landlord James Taylor had arrived at the cottage shortly afterwards and Milborough had come to the door looking 'very poorly', which Taylor had put down to the shock of the child's accident. Milborough asked Taylor for some oil for the burn but Taylor recommended that she applied some raw potato to the area.

Within two days of her confinement, Milborough was back at work in the fields as if nothing had happened. If asked about the baby, she insisted that her child had been born dead and that Taylor had buried it for her.

The news of his alleged involvement in the concealment of the body of a child soon reached Taylor's ears and he went straight to confront Milborough about her story. Milborough told him that, on 24 June, she felt very bad and that 'some blood had come from her'. She admitted to Taylor that she had given birth to a dead baby, which she had subsequently buried in a field owned by his cousin, John Taylor.

James Taylor was horrified by what he heard, so much so that he went to the village constable, Samuel Griffiths, and reported the conversation to him. Having first interviewed Sarah Scrivens, Griffiths arrested Milborough Trilloe on 7 July.

Milborough admitted to Griffiths that she had given birth, telling the constable that the child had been born dead and that she had buried it. Griffiths asked her to show him where she had put her baby and Milborough led him to a ditch where she said she had dug a hole for the infant's corpse. Although the ground appeared solid and undisturbed to Griffiths, he fetched a spade and dug down at the spot where Milborough assured him her child's body was buried. He found nothing.

Milborough however insisted that she had buried her baby at that very spot, suggesting that the infant had probably 'wasted away'. Griffiths asked her several times to tell him exactly where she had concealed the body, pointing out that she was not helping her case by withholding the information. Nevertheless, Milborough refused to reveal any more about the whereabouts of her child and eventually Griffiths was forced to scour the entire area around her cottage, looking for soil that had been disturbed.

He found what he was looking for in a corner of James Taylor's garden. A small patch of earth looked to have been recently turned and when Griffiths scraped away the topsoil with his spade, he soon uncovered the body of a baby. Griffiths placed the dead child in a basket, which he carried to local magistrate, James Palmer.

The tiny body was examined by doctors who determined that it was a full-term baby girl. The colour of the child's lungs and the fact that its chest appeared 'arched' suggested that it had been born alive. The doctors noted what they described as 'marks of violence' on the child's neck.

Confronted with this information, Milborough Trilloe changed her story, telling Griffiths that she had given birth at between five and six o'clock, shortly after Sarah Scrivens had left for work. The child had been born alive and, after the birth, Milborough had been in so much pain that she had unwittingly caught hold of its neck with her hands. The baby gasped two or three times and then died. The constable immediately arrested her on suspicion of murdering her baby and she was placed in the custody of James Palmer.

Having further examined the baby's makeshift grave, Griffiths then came to the conclusion that digging it would have required considerable effort and began to doubt whether a woman who had so recently given birth would have been strong enough to do it. He therefore arrested James Taylor and he too was placed in Palmer's custody where, on seeing Milborough Trilloe, he remarked, 'You have brought me into a fine scrape.'

Fortunately for Taylor, there was absolutely no evidence to connect him with either the death of the baby or the concealment of its body and he was soon released. Meanwhile, an inquest was opened into the infant's death, at which the coroner's jury returned a verdict of 'wilful murder' against Milborough Trilloe, who was committed for trial at the next Herefordshire Assizes.

The trial opened on 3 August 1842 before Mr Justice Erskine, with Mr Greaves and Mr Barrett prosecuting and Mr W.H. Cooke defending.

Details of the proceedings in both the local and the national newspapers of the time are unfortunately sketchy, with the *Hereford Times* reporting: 'The evidence of the medical gentlemen was next taken but much of it was, of course, of a nature unsuited for publication, neither would it be understood by the general reader.' The only evidence that the paper thought fit for its readership was that the doctors who had examined the baby believed that the cause of its death was strangulation and that something flat had been pressed against the child's windpipe for so long and with such force that '...even after death it did not assume its usual circular form.'

The court heard from Sarah Scrivens, James Taylor and his cousin John. John Taylor testified to seeing Milborough at the cottage at about eight o'clock on the morning of 24 June, at which point she was fully dressed and definitely not pregnant, although she appeared shocked and frightened by the accident to Sarah's child. Constable Griffiths gave his account of unearthing the dead child, telling the court that there had been a lump on the baby's throat and strenuously denying the defence counsel's allegation that he had damaged the body in the course of its exhumation. The prosecution also called midwife Mrs Baldwin to testify that she had not been called to assist the defendant in her confinement.

Counsel for the defence, Mr Cooke, contended that Milborough Trilloe had been almost beside herself with the agony of childbirth and had simply not realised what she was doing when she grasped the child's throat. Cooke told the court that, under the circumstances, he didn't believe that his client should even have been charged with manslaughter, let alone murder, since the baby's death had been the result of an involuntary action on the part of a woman who was half-crazed with pain.

It was a testimony to Cooke's impassioned speech in his client's defence that the jury found it necessary to deliberate their verdict for almost ninety minutes. It was, of course, an all male jury, none of whom would have personally experienced the pain of childbirth and they returned to court to pronounce Milborough Trilloe

'Guilty' of the wilful murder of her baby, although they added a recommendation for mercy.

On hearing the verdict, Milborough '... became affected with spasms to such an extent that she was totally unconscious of what was going on.' One of the medical witnesses, Dr Bull, went to her aid and, by administering a restorative, brought her back to consciousness in time to hear the judge pronounce the death sentence.

In the course of the trial, the counsel for the defence had objected to one particular piece of the medical evidence, although the newspapers of the time are reticent to give details of exactly what that objection was. However, they note that the resulting point of law would be placed before fifteen judges for their consideration, which, according to Mr Justice Erskine, would cause a delay of some weeks. Telling Milborough that he personally held out no hopes that the sentence of death would not ultimately be carried out, Erskine urged her to prepare to appear before her Maker with deep repentance and steadfast faith.

The date of the execution was provisionally set for 24 November 1842 but, after more than a year of legal wrangling, it was announced in November 1843 that Her Majesty the Queen had exercised her royal clemency and, as a consequence, Milborough Trilloe's death sentence had been commuted to one of transportation for life.

6

'... A SUCCESSION OF DIABOLICAL OUTRAGES THAT ARE A DISGRACE TO ANY COUNTRY OR PEOPLE'

Eaton Bishop, 1843

In the 1840s, the parish of Madley, which lies approximately six miles to the west of Hereford, was beset by a rash of arson attacks. These were particularly frequent during 1843, when it was reported in the contemporary newspapers: 'Madley continues to be the scene of a succession of diabolical outrages that are a disgrace to any country or people.' Between 9 March and 12 August, there were no less than seven serious fires, all in farm buildings, which caused considerable damage to both property and stored crops and the loss of the lives of several farm animals. 'The secrecy in which these nefarious schemes are planned and executed is astonishing,' reported the *Gloucester Journal*, adding that separate rewards ranging from £100 to £300 had been offered for the detention of the 'marauders'.

At some time during the night of 8/9 November, the 'marauders' struck in the neighbouring parish of Eaton Bishop, at the property of Mr Bennett of Wormhill. Bennett's carter woke to find his room illuminated by a bright orange glare. Thinking that the house was on fire, he raised the alarm and his fellow servants seized what they could of their personal possessions and ran downstairs and out of the house. It was only when they got outside that they realised that only the hay and straw ricks and the farm outbuildings were ablaze.

Mr Bennett immediately sent a messenger to Hereford for a fire engine and meanwhile set the servants to work moving horses and machinery out of the buildings. The messenger arrived at the fire station in Hereford at ten minutes to two in the morning and roused the fire superintendent, George Adams. Adams and his crew set off for Bennett's farm straight away but, by the time they arrived, four hay ricks, two corn ricks, the cow house, cider house and mill and a barn had all been totally consumed by the flames.

Bennett's neighbours had been trying to douse the fire for some time but their efforts were hampered by a lack of water, as was the fire engine. It was ten o'clock in the morning before the fire was completely extinguished and a closer inspection could be made of the burned buildings.

A few days before the fire, Mr Bennett had been approached by a man named Peregrine Morgan, a travelling tinker, who was well known in the area and went by the name of 'Tinker Perry'. Morgan asked Bennett's permission to sleep in one of his barns and Bennett told him that he was welcome to do so. Now, in the wake of the all-consuming fire, Tinker Perry was nowhere to be found.

The *Gloucester Journal* was widely misquoted in several contemporary newspapers as having reported that the tinker had managed to escape the blaze and was in Hereford Infirmary, being treated for serious burns. Quite how reporters came by that information can only be a matter of conjecture, as Morgan had actually suffered a far worse fate.

As investigators combed the ruined buildings, they searched the pig barn and discovered something that was definitely not porcine in origin lying among the cremated bodies of ten dead pigs. At first, nobody was quite sure if what had been discovered was the remains of a human being or not, since the fierce heat and flames had completely charred the body, which was missing its head and the majority of its torso from the waist upwards. Eventually doctors were able to determine that the blackened remains were those of a man, who they presumed to be Peregrine Morgan. Due to his location in the building, it was assumed that Morgan had awakened to find the barn in which he was sleeping on fire and had tried to escape but been beaten back by the heat and perished in the flames.

An inquest was held into Peregrine Morgan's death before coroner Mr Nicholas Lanwarne, where it was determined that Morgan had retired for the night at about nine o'clock on 8 November. The fire had broken out about five hours later and was unmistakeably the work of an arsonist.

After some deliberation, the coroner's jury returned a verdict of 'wilful murder against some person or persons unknown in having feloniously set fire to certain buildings thereby causing the death of the said Peregrine Morgan.'

In spite of stringent investigations by both the police and the Hereford District Coroner, Mr Evans, the spate of fire-raising in Herefordshire continued long after the death of Peregrine Morgan, especially in the area around Madley. In one particular incident in 1849, farmer Mr Preece of Newton lost 200 bushels of wheat in the straw, a threshing machine and a large number of hens and the newspapers of the time reported that the people who gathered to watch the spectacle feasted on freshly roasted chicken.

Numerous people were arrested and subsequently tried for starting the fires but they normally proved to be individuals with a supposed grudge against the affected farmers. One such man was John Mutlow, who had made threats against his employer after being sacked, although Mutlow was later acquitted, having satisfactorily proved that he was ill at home at the time the fire started.

In 1849, farmer John Price was tried for starting a fire at the Madley farm of John Smith, in which numerous farm buildings were gutted and five horses and cows burned to death. At his trial before Mr Justice Erle, Price was acquitted due to lack of evidence against him, but he was immediately followed into the dock by fourteen-year-old John Jones, who was accused of setting fire to farm buildings in Preston-on-Wye on 23 April 1849. The resulting conflagration consumed two barns, several sheds, outbuildings and stables, causing damage amounting to a total of £1,200.

Jones was employed as a stable boy at the farm which was owned by the Dean and Chapter of the Cathedral of Hereford and tenanted by Mr Davis. Davis had been dissatisfied with Jones' execution of his duties in the stables and had demoted him to manual labour, replacing him with another boy.

Jones had gone to view the ruins of John Smith's farm at Madley and had recognised what he believed to be an ideal way of gaining revenge on his master for his demotion. Having made a full confession, both to Mr Davis' sister and later to the police, Jones was found 'Guilty', although the jury added a recommendation of mercy on the grounds of his youth. He was sentenced to be transported for fifteen years.

The fire in which Peregrine Morgan lost his life was undoubtedly started deliberately, since spent matches were found close to the ruins of the outbuildings. As far as investigators could establish, there was nobody with a particular grudge against Mr Bennett and certainly nobody with any possible motive to murder Peregrine Morgan.

At that time, Hereford was not the only county to be experiencing unprecedented incendiary attacks. On 30 December 1843, *The Times* cites similar outbreaks in Bedfordshire, Essex and Kent, as well as reporting a further arson attack in Herefordshire, this time at stables close to Hereford Pig Market. The newspaper theorised that the fires may have been deliberately set by agricultural labourers in an effort to destroy – or at least discourage the use of – the mechanised implements that were gradually taking away their livelihoods. In fact, it is most probable that whoever set the fire at Eaton Bishop didn't even know that there was anybody sleeping in the barn at the time and merely intended to damage property rather than to take a life. Whoever that person was, they undoubtedly carried the death of Tinker Perry on their conscience to the grave, since nobody was ever charged with either arson or murder in relation to the fire that claimed his life.

7

'THOMAS HAS A SPELL AND I MUST GET IT REMOVED, COST WHAT IT MIGHT'

Brilley, 1848

On 25 October 1848, Mary Price paid a visit to her cousin, Elizabeth Whitford, at her home in Brilley. Mary arrived just as Elizabeth and her husband, Thomas, were sitting down for their evening meal and Thomas politely invited Mary to join them, fetching a cup and saucer and pouring tea for her.

Thomas worked as a drover and cattle dealer and his job involved him spending long periods of time away from home. He had recently returned after a month away and, on his return, Elizabeth had noticed some worrying changes in his behaviour. The Whitfords were apparently very happily married and Thomas was normally a good husband and provider. However at the same time, there were rumours that he was addicted to drink and he was certainly prone to bouts of 'strangeness' on occasions. To Mary Price, his manner seemed a little unusual that evening. He ate very little and had to be dissuaded from drinking his tea scalding hot, his wife urging him several times to allow it to cool slightly so that he would not burn his mouth.

Fifteen years earlier, Thomas had experienced another bout of 'strangeness' and now Elizabeth had grave concerns for her own safety. She had already said as much to a neighbour, Richard Clarke, telling him that Thomas was out of his mind and that her life was in danger, although Clarke had dismissed her concerns, having spoken to Thomas, and found him to be 'sane and shrewd'. Elizabeth had also voiced

32

her fears to Elizabeth Wanklin, Mary's daughter, telling her, 'Thomas has a spell and I must get it removed, cost what it might.' Now, Elizabeth Whitford told Mary in a whispered conversation that her husband was in 'an odd state of mind', just as he had been fifteen years ago. Yet Mary had no real concerns for her cousin as she left the Whitfords' home at about seven o'clock that evening, since the couple appeared to be on their normal good terms.

Elizabeth told Mary that she was intending to go to Hay-on-Wye market the next day and Mary had some goods that she wanted taking there. She promised to drop them off for Elizabeth to take with her the following morning. However, when Mary arrived at her cousin's cottage at ten o'clock, she found the door firmly closed. Mary tried the latch but could not get the door to open, so she shouted her cousin's name to try and attract her attention.

At first, there was no reply but when Mary continued to call out, Thomas eventually answered from inside the cottage, 'Betty is dead on the bed. She cannot come to you.'

Horrified, Mary told him to open the door but Thomas told her that it was locked and he couldn't find the key. Mary was an elderly lady and breaking down the door was beyond her physical capabilities. Telling Thomas to wait there, she rushed off in search of some help.

She returned two hours later with two men, Richard Clarke and another neighbour, John Powell. Since Thomas still professed himself unable to find the key, the two men managed to force the door open and were met with a terrible sight. Elizabeth Whitford lay on the kitchen floor completely naked and quite dead. Her head had been literally smashed to pieces and the room was liberally spattered with blood, brain tissue and fragments of bone. In the midst of the carnage, pacing relentlessly up and down, was forty-five-year-old Thomas Whitford, who insisted to the horrified neighbours that he had successfully battled the great Goddess Diana in the depths of a bottomless pit. He seemed to have no understanding of the fact that the dead woman on the kitchen floor was actually his wife. 'If I had known it was my own wife, I should not have done it,' he told John Powell sadly when the truth finally dawned on him.

The police and a doctor were called and, realising that he could do nothing to help Elizabeth, surgeon Mr Woodcock from Hay-on-Wye concentrated on speaking to her husband, who was by then rambling incoherently. When he was arrested for the wilful murder of his wife, Thomas insisted on reciting Psalm 109, which was universally known as 'the cursing psalm', repeated since medieval times by dying men who wished to bring about the destruction and demise of their enemies:

Let his days be few: and let another take his office. Let his children be fatherless: and his wife a widow. Let his children be vagabonds and beg their bread. Let the extortioner consume all that he hath, and let the stranger spoil his labour. Let his posterity be destroyed: and in the next generation let his name be clean put out.

On his way to prison, Thomas admitted killing his wife, telling the constable escorting him that, in doing so, he had been fulfilling the commands of the Scriptures.

Not surprisingly, a post-mortem examination conducted by surgeons Mr Woodcock and Mr Terry on what remained of Elizabeth Whitford found the cause of her death to be her terrible head injuries. The remains of a broken ladder had been found in the kitchen of her cottage, covered in clotted blood, brain tissue and hair, and it was obvious that this had been the weapon used by Thomas to batter Elizabeth to death. An inquest was opened, at which the coroner's jury found a verdict of 'wilful murder against Thomas Whitford', although they expressed their opinion that he was unsound of mind at the time of the murder. However, even though he might privately have agreed with the jury's concerns, it was not the coroner's place to investigate Whitford's state of mind and he was committed on a coroner's warrant to stand trial at the next Hereford Assizes.

The trial opened before Mr Baron Platt on 24 March 1849, with Mr Skinner and Mr Davis prosecuting and Mr W.H. Cooke defending Thomas Whitford, who now seemed distraught at the realisation that he had killed his wife. The results of the trial were a foregone conclusion with Mr Cooke suggesting to the jury that, at the time he committed the 'dreadful act', Whitford was apparently not a responsible being. The jury concurred, needing only a very brief deliberation to return their verdict of 'Not Guilty on the grounds of insanity' and Whitford was ordered by the judge to be detained during Her Majesty's pleasure.

8

'WE DON'T WANT ANY ROW HERE TONIGHT'

Hereford, 1855

Bowsey Lane (now Wall Street) in Hereford was once the city's 'red light district' and almost every house on the street was a brothel. In 1855, a new sewerage works was being built to serve the city of Hereford and, especially on Saturday nights, Bowsey Lane acted like a magnet to the construction workers, who had plenty of money in their pockets to spend on the prostitutes who congregated there. On Saturday, 29 September, a group of eight workers from the sewerage works went out for a night on the town and, after consuming vast quantities of drink, they headed for Bowsey Lane in search of some female company.

One of the men, John Wilson, met prostitute Hannah Downes and negotiated a price to spend the rest of the night with her. Hannah took John back to a brothel in Bowsey Lane, run by Sarah Lloyd and her boyfriend, Charles Holmes. Wilson and Hannah retired to her bed, where Wilson eventually fell asleep. He woke suddenly to find Hannah rifling through the pockets of the clothes he had hastily discarded earlier. As soon as Hannah realised that Wilson was awake, she fled, taking with her all of her client's money.

Wilson leaped out of bed in a rage, intent on chasing after Hannah and getting his money back. However, as well as his money, Hannah had also taken his boots and his frock coat. Wilson began to bellow for Hannah to come back with his clothes and his shouting disturbed Sarah Lloyd, who was sleeping elsewhere in the house with Holmes.

Sarah rushed to investigate the source of the commotion and, on confronting the furious John Wilson, she ordered him out of her house. Together, she and Holmes, who was very drunk at the time, manhandled the truculent Wilson out through

Hereford High Town, 1950. (Author's collection)

the front door. However Wilson, who was equally drunk, had paid for a night's stay with Hannah and was not happy to be cheated out of something that he had paid good money for. He violently resisted Holmes and Sarah Lloyd, lashing out with his fists and feet and pulling out great clumps of hair from both of their heads.

The fight spilled out onto the street, where Sarah Lloyd's cries of 'Murder!' soon attracted a crowd of people, including the men with whom Wilson worked. All of them ploughed into the mêlée with gusto, and soon Holmes was on the receiving end of a severe beating, which left him bloodied and bruised and might well have killed him had a neighbour not waded in to the fight to assist him and dragged him back indoors.

The 'navvies' were left standing on the street, shouting and cursing and threatening extreme violence to those who were still on their doorsteps awaiting the next phase of the evening's entertainment. One of these was prostitute Priscilla Morgan, who lived in the house next door with her boyfriend.

While Priscilla's boyfriend went to alert the police, Priscilla made a vain attempt to defuse the violent situation, saying to the men, 'There's good men, go home. We don't want any row here tonight.' Rather than calming the men as Priscilla had intended, her polite request seemed to inflame them still further and one of them ran at her wielding a heavy rolling pin, with which he had armed himself at the start of the fight. In front of numerous witnesses, he swung the rolling pin at Priscilla, hitting her hard on her left eye. Priscilla immediately fell backwards, hitting her head on the bricks at the edge of the door as she did so and dropping senseless to the floor. As soon as they saw her fall, one of the navvies said that they should leave because the police would soon be arriving, at which all of them took to their heels and ran away.

Priscilla lay unconscious on the doorstep of her home. Her neighbours picked her up and carried her upstairs to her bedroom, where they began to apply cold cloths to her wounds, while somebody ran for a doctor to attend her. Dr Bull arrived very quickly and, in view of the seriousness of Priscilla's injuries, he summoned local surgeon Mr Hanbury. Priscilla's face was black and blue. She had a large contused wound on the left-hand side of her head, along with two lacerations in her face, one of which had penetrated completely through her left cheek into her mouth. Her left eye was completely shut and her jaw was also swollen, several of her teeth having been knocked out or loosened. Hanbury arranged for Priscilla to be taken to hospital and, although everything possible was done to try and save her life, she died early on the following Tuesday morning. At a post-mortem examination it was discovered that her death was due to swelling and compression of the brain, beneath a skull fracture on the left side of her head.

There had been numerous witnesses to the fight, including two militia men and a policeman, PC Mansell, who had happened upon the scene and immediately gone off to fetch reinforcements. Thus it was a relatively simple task for the police to identify the navvies who had been involved and they soon arrested Robert Scott (46), a foreman, and labourers John Wilson (24), Henry Williams (20), William Higgins (22) and James Ford (25). Another one of the gang, Charles Smith (22), was later apprehended in Worcester.

An inquest was opened into Priscilla's death by the city coroner and attended by those workers who were currently under arrest for her murder. Having heard from several witnesses, the coroner quickly discharged Charles Smith, who was able to provide an alibi that was confirmed by two people. The coroner's jury returned a verdict of manslaughter on the five remaining men, who were committed for trial at the next Assizes on a coroner's warrant.

However, no sooner had the inquest terminated than the Mayor of Hereford announced that he disputed the coroner's verdict and demanded the re-arrest of Charles Smith. The Mayor had all six men brought up before magistrates and the charge against them was upgraded to one of wilful murder, the magistrates having determined that there was a case to answer on the capital charge.

Although the police now had most of the men in their custody, they were well aware that they had not yet caught them all. John Green (30) was captured a few days later and he too was charged with the wilful murder of Priscilla Morgan. Yet the man who had actually struck Priscilla with the rolling pin had not been apprehended, even though a large reward had been authorised for anyone giving information leading to his capture. Steven Williams (27) appeared to have left Hereford in a great hurry in the immediate aftermath of the brutal attack on Priscilla and the police had no idea of his whereabouts. Unfortunately for Williams, he had a particularly distinctive appearance – he generally went by the nickname 'Whitelock', owing to the fact that he had a large patch of pure white in his otherwise dark brown hair. It was this feature that enabled those who had watched the fight to identify him as the man who had hit Priscilla and it was the same feature that led to his eventual arrest in Kidderminster.

Williams was taken to Hereford by train and brought before magistrates on his arrival. The magistrates then summoned witness Josiah Underwood, who had been drinking in the Three Crowns Inn on the night of 29 September and, in the early hours of the following morning, had heard Sarah Lloyd's desperate screams of 'Murder!'.

He ran the 200 yards or so to Bowsey Lane, where he saw a large, angry group of men kicking at the door, obviously trying to get at Charles Holmes, who had by then been taken inside by his neighbour. Underwood heard Priscilla urging the men to go home, at which Steven Williams flew at her, a rolling pin held in his right hand. Underwood told the magistrates that he was positive that Williams was the man he had seen, on account of the streak of white hair. Williams hit Priscilla hard on the left side of her face, at which she fell, striking her head on the bricks at the side of the door.

Thus Williams became the eighth navvy to be charged with the wilful murder of Priscilla Morgan and, in the eyes of the law, although he was apparently the only one among the men to have actually struck the deceased, all bore an equal responsibility for her murder.

The trial was scheduled to commence on 15 December but before it began, the case was placed before the Grand Jury. The role of the Grand Jury was to decide whether or not there was sufficient evidence to actually try the case and their decision was reached by hearing the evidence for the prosecution. In the murder of Priscilla Morgan, the Grand Jury decided that the prosecution had insufficient evidence to justify trying the defendants on the charges of wilful murder against them. However, charges of murder and manslaughter by coroner's juries did not need the approval of the Grand Jury. These cases automatically went to trial and, since the original inquest verdict was one of manslaughter against the defendants and they had been committed to stand trial for manslaughter on the coroner's warrant, the charges against all eight defendants were reduced from wilful murder to manslaughter.

Thus, the eight men, all of whom pleaded 'Not Guilty' to the charge of manslaughter, appeared before Mr Justice Williams. Mr Scotland and Mr Cleave prosecuted the case, while Mr Skinner and Mr Matthews defended.

Mr Scotland related the events of the early morning of 30 September and informed the jury that it was their job to decide whether any one of the prisoners was concerned with causing Priscilla Morgan's death. He explained that, if the men were engaged in a common purpose of rioting and disturbance and somebody died as a result of this unlawful violence then, in the eyes of the law, all who were present and taking part in the disturbance would be equally culpable for that death.

Scotland then informed the court that the prisoner John Wilson had been seen engaged in a fight with Sarah Lloyd and Charles Holmes outside the house they occupied with Hannah Downes and another prostitute, Maria Hunt. Later, Steven Williams, Charles Smith and James Ford had joined him, the four men beating Charles Holmes almost senseless, after which Williams was seen hitting Priscilla Morgan with a rolling pin, a blow which ultimately resulted in her death. By this time, all eight of the navvies were heavily involved in the fight, which continued until they saw Priscilla fall to the ground, when they hurriedly fled before the police could arrive.

The prosecution then called a series of twenty witnesses to provide their recollections of the night's events. Unfortunately, the fight had been a chaotic affair and had occurred in the middle of the night, when it had, of course, been dark. Thus there was an amount of discrepancy between the accounts of the witnesses, some of whom directly contradicted the others on cross-examination by the defence.

In addition, most of the eyewitnesses were what the newspapers of the day described as 'people of the lowest possible description'. Many were 'common prostitutes or brothel keepers' and one man actually owned ten houses of ill repute on the notorious Bowsey Lane. The defence managed to portray the majority of the witnesses as the lowest forms of human life while, at the same time, building up a picture of the defendants as respectable, honest and hard-working men.

The defence team contended that little or no reliance could be placed on the 'tainted and untrustworthy' evidence of the residents of Bowsey Lane, leaving what they referred to as just four reliable, decent witnesses. These were the two militia men, who had actually seen very little, and PC Mansell, who had witnessed the fight but had already left the scene to fetch reinforcements by the time the fatal blow was struck. Thus, the entire case for the prosecution ultimately rested on the evidence of Josiah Underwood, who was unshakeable in his testimony that he had seen Williams, with his distinctive white hair, striking the blow that killed Priscilla Morgan.

It was perhaps too much to expect the jury to find all of the defendants guilty of an offence that was committed by just one man and, after a brief deliberation, they returned to pronounce all eight of the accused 'Not Guilty'. The verdict was greeted with a round of applause from the spectators in the court as, to the delight and obvious relief of the defendants, the judge discharged them.

Thus, the murder of Priscilla Morgan, who had done nothing more than make an inoffensive remark to try and defuse a violent fight, went unpunished. One cannot help but wonder if the outcome of the case might have been different had Priscilla been a respectable young woman rather than a common prostitute, or if Steven Williams alone had stood trial for her brutal murder.

Note: James Ford is alternatively named Thomas Ford in some contemporary accounts of the case.

9

'IT WAS THE CRUELLEST SIGHT THAT ANYBODY EVER SAW'

Ledbury, 1859

In May 1859, Harriet Baker was still grieving for her husband, who had died only six weeks earlier. Harriet lived at a house in Ledbury, part of which was used as the offices of Mr Edward Masefield, a local solicitor, who employed Harriet as his 'office keeper'. During the working day, Masefield also employed five clerks but, once the offices were closed, Harriet was the only occupant of the building, with the exception of Elizabeth Paine, an eight-year-old girl, who sometimes stayed with her. It was normal practice for one of the clerks, Richard Dew, to lock up the premises every evening and afterwards take the keys to his employer's home.

On Tuesday 17 May, Dew locked up at about ten past eight in the evening. Harriet was visited by a female friend, Charlotte Jackson, who stayed until just before ten o'clock and, on leaving, heard Harriet locking the outer door behind her. Harriet had rigged up a system of bells behind each of the doors to alert her to any attempt at a break in. However, on the morning of 18 May, neighbours noticed that Harriet wasn't up and about at her normal time.

Concerned, the neighbours threw a hail of small stones at her bedroom window and, when this drew no response, were on the verge of breaking in when John Isaac Jones appeared with a key to the back door. Jones, another of Masefield's clerks, lodged next door to the office and told the assembled neighbours that he had found the key lying on the gravel path under the office window.

Church Lane, Ledbury. (Author's collection)

The Feathers Hotel, Ledbury. (Author's collection)

Jones opened the door and he and several of the neighbours went inside. In Mrs Baker's living room, a rug was disturbed as though a scuffle had taken place on it and the doors to several of the rooms were open, although they had been closed the previous evening. By now, it was obvious to everyone that something bad had happened to Harriet Baker but nothing could have prepared the neighbours for what they found when they opened the door to Mr Masefield's office. Thomas Bowkett, a shoemaker and John Jones' landlord, was later to say tearfully, 'It was the cruellest sight that anybody ever saw.'

The room was filled with a dense cloud of black, malodorous smoke. As the smoke cleared slightly, it was possible to see the body of Harriet Baker lying on the floor, her feet about a yard from the door. Harriet's dark brown hair was 'thrown back in wild dishevelment', revealing a large bruise on her forehead. Her face was a livid purple in colour, her eyes bulged and the marks of strangulation were plainly visible on her throat. Most of Harriet's torso had been consumed by fire, which had left only her head, lower legs and feet unscathed. The fire, which was still smouldering, had burned through the coconut matting and floorboards in two places beneath the body. More horrific still was the fact that, in Harriet's bedroom, Elizabeth Paine was still sleeping peacefully, totally unaware of the carnage that had occurred within just a few feet of her bed.

Such was the position in which the body lay that it was not possible for Harriet to have fallen. Thus it was obvious that someone had murdered the unfortunate widow and then moved her body into the office before starting a fire, presumably in the hope of destroying all evidence that a murder had been committed.

Naturally the police and a doctor were summoned. The doctors, Mr Griffin and Mr Wood, later made a post-mortem examination and discovered that Harriet Baker had been strangled, most probably with the cord with a running noose and slip knot that was found partially burned beneath her body. Mrs Baker's tongue was swollen, her lungs were congested and she had two large bruises on her head. The doctors surmised that, unless more than one person had been involved in her murder, Harriet had almost certainly been hit in order to stun her or render her unconscious, to allow her killer to slip the noose over her head. Harriet's stomach contained a small quantity of food and the doctors estimated that she had died three or four hours after eating. They confirmed that she had not been violated but believed that she had still been alive when she was set on fire.

On examination of the house, the police found that none of the outside doors appeared to have been tampered with, leading them to believe that Harriet had either known her killer and let him or her into the house or that the killer had concealed him or herself in the building before it was locked up for the night. Harriet's alarm bell had been removed from the back door, through which her killer had obviously escaped, locking it behind him or her and afterwards discarding the keys on the gravel path. Several drawers in Mr Masefield's office had been pried open, as had the safe, which had been forced using tools from the house belonging to the late Mr Baker. Numerous items had been stolen including cheques, some gold and silver coins, a quantity of postage stamps and two £5 notes.

The police spoke to Charlotte Jackson, who told them that Mrs Baker's living room was not as it had been when she left it shortly before ten o'clock. A white tablecloth had since been laid on the table, which now bore a jug of water, a knife, a sugar basin and two used glasses that smelled as if they might once have contained spirits. There was also a candlestick with a nearly new candle, which hadn't been there while Charlotte was visiting. A silver watch hung on a nail over the fireplace and Mrs Baker's widow's cap was on the floor. The police were unable to understand why nobody had heard any sounds of a disturbance – Elizabeth had slept through the night, while neighbour John Bowkett, who had retired to bed at ten o'clock, had heard nothing at all, in spite of the fact that only a thin partition wall separated his bedroom from Mr Masefield's office. In addition, nobody had seen any lights showing at the house.

The police soon began to suspect that the murder had been committed by someone who was very familiar with the premises and who had thus been able to move around in the darkness without needing a candle to light his or her way.

In addition, the only drawers that had been forced were those that usually contained cash.

It was customary for all money received at Masefield's office to be entered into a ledger and, in the two days prior to the murder, there had been two large payments made, totalling more than £300. All of the solicitor's five clerks were aware that these payments had been received and yet only two – a Mr W.G. Woodward and Richard Dew – knew that the money had actually been deposited in the bank on the day of the murder. As two of the remaining three clerks were Mr Masefield's sons, Henry and William, the police turned their attention to the fifth, John Isaac Jones.

Jones had worked for Mr Masefield for two and a half years and, according to his employer, had always been excellent at his job. Masefield knew little of Jones' background, although he believed that he was an American citizen who had worked in Australia and, indeed, the reference that Jones presented when he started work for Masefield came from an Australian company, even though Jones had come to Ledbury from Birmingham. Other than that, the only thing that was remarkable about Jones was that he had a cork leg, which he told people was the result of an attack on him by bush rangers in the Australian gold fields.

In reality, Jones' life was not as exotic as he would have people believe and he had never even been out of England. Even so, he kept two diaries, one detailing his real life and the other his fantasy life. Having lost his leg in a childhood accident, he had been a pauper at the workhouse in Birmingham. For a short time in 1856 he had been elevated to the position of office assistant to the workhouse master, Charles Cooper, for which he was paid the sum of 15s a week and his board. From September to October 1856, he had also acted as schoolmaster at the workhouse while the regular teacher was ill.

Jones had then applied to the Ledbury workhouse for the position of porter, bringing with him glowing references from Birmingham. However, what the management at Birmingham did not realise at the time was that Jones was having an illicit relationship with an inmate, Mary Jackson, who was expecting his child. Mary was led to believe that she would be moving to Ledbury workhouse with Jones but, in the event, the couple quarrelled and Mary returned to Birmingham, where she later gave birth to a son. She hadn't seen Jones since and had received nothing from him in the way of support for her child. (Sadly, the boy died in Birmingham workhouse two months before his second birthday.)

Prior to his arrival in Birmingham, Jones was employed as a solicitor's clerk in his native Burnham in Somerset. While there, he began courting one of two sisters, announcing his intention of marrying her. When his then employer heard that there was to be a wedding, he gave Jones a gift of money. However, Jones took advantage of his fiancée's affection for him and seduced her, presumably leaving her pregnant. Not content with one sister, he then 'made an attempt on the virtue' of the other and was forced to leave the area in a hurry to escape the consequences of his actions, taking his employer's generous wedding gift with him.

As the police and local magistrates looked more closely at John Jones as a possible suspect, the circumstantial evidence against him mounted. Jones knew the premises well enough to move around them comfortably in the dark and was aware of where the money was kept. He knew of the two large payments recently received but did not know that the money had already been banked and was no longer in the office. Because of his cork leg, Jones rarely went upstairs at work and thus there were drawers where money was normally kept, of which he was not aware. These drawers had not been disturbed during the robbery.

Jones was known to be friendly with Harriet Baker, who often did his mending for him. His quarterly salary was last paid in March and, immediately before the murder, Jones was short of money. However, after the murder he had plenty of ready cash and when the police searched his rooms they found £10 in gold, along with numerous other coins. Stamps had been among the items stolen and, on 18 May, Jones had repaid the loan of a shilling from Richard Dew with stamps. Even having repaid his loan, Jones still had plenty more stamps in his possession, some of which seemed to have been torn from the same sheet as those left in Masefield's office.

On the morning after the murder, before the discovery of Harriet's body, Jones had risen unusually early and cleaned his shoes in what was described as the 'shoe house' at his lodgings. On a path close to the shoe house, a small paper packet of coins was found, which it could be proved were part of the haul taken from Masefield's office.

Jones normally visited the Bell Hotel between seven and eight o'clock every evening and drank a pint of beer but, on the night of 17 May, he returned at around ten o'clock for some gin and water. The following morning, before Harriet's body was discovered, Jones was back in the pub. He looked very ill and complained that he hadn't slept well, although landlady Jane Cole was later to say that he always looked ill in the mornings. He brought with him a soda bottle, which he asked to be filled with half a pint of brandy. Later that evening, he was back at the pub, drinking brandy and water.

Yet perhaps the most damning evidence against Jones was a bludgeon found in a chest in his room, which exactly matched the bruises on Harriet Baker's head.

An inquest was opened by coroner Mr Underwood, at which the jury eventually recorded a verdict of 'murder by person or persons unknown'. However, the belief that John Jones was that 'person unknown' was getting stronger by the minute and Jones was eventually arrested and charged with the murder. After appearing before magistrates, he was committed for trial at the next Hereford Assizes. Once it was generally known that Jones was the chief suspect for Harriet's murder, the townspeople of Ledbury began to clamour for the exhumation of her husband, who had died following a sudden illness that had unexpectedly struck him immediately after he had kept company with Jones.

It was widely rumoured that the coroner had issued a warrant for the exhumation to take place but Mr Masefield, who acted as clerk to the magistrates, quickly quashed the rumours. The authorities were apparently happy to believe the doctor who had attended Mr Baker and stated that there was absolutely no evidence to suggest that he might have been poisoned. Thus, the magistrates refused to apply to the coroner for a warrant unless the townspeople were prepared to raise £100 themselves to defray the expenses. Not surprisingly, the matter was quickly dropped.

With the Assizes due to begin at the start of August, police continued their enquiries into the murder and, in late July, made a further search of the bedroom at Mr Bowkett's house, formerly occupied by John Jones. Although the room had been thoroughly searched before, the police now noticed some ashes in the grate. They were carefully collected and examined under a microscope and found to be the burned remains of banknotes, although the police could not say with absolute certainty that they were the actual £5 notes stolen from the solicitor's office.

Nevertheless, it was yet another piece of circumstantial evidence against John Jones, who appeared in the dock at the opening of his trial on 2 August looking pale, nervous and very agitated. The trial was presided over by Mr Justice Byles, with Mr Skinner QC, Mr W.H. Cooke and Mr Powell prosecuting. Mr Huddlestone and Mr James handled Jones' defence.

The prosecution maintained that the presence of the tablecloth and two glasses on Harriet Baker's table suggested that she had entertained another friend on the evening of her murder, after Charlotte Jackson had left. John Jones was a friend of Harriet's and it was easy to imagine him tapping on her door to collect the pair of trousers she had been mending for him and being invited inside. The prosecution then went on to list all the evidence against Jones point by point, admitting that, although largely circumstantial, it all seemed to lead to only one conclusion – that John Isaac Jones was Harriet Baker's killer.

Yet, however persuasive the evidence against Jones might have seemed, it was, as the counsel for the prosecution admitted, only circumstantial. And while Jones was undoubtedly a teller of tall tales, the prosecution were unable to convince the jury that he was also a murderer as, after deliberating for an hour, they acquitted him. On hearing the 'Not Guilty' verdict, Jones promptly collapsed with a seizure and it was with some difficulty that he was removed from the dock and discharged from court, leaving the murder of Harriet Baker to remain unsolved.

Note: Thomas Bowkett is alternatively named Thomas Boycutt in some contemporary newspaper accounts of the murder.

10

'I SHALL SAY NOTHING'

Ullingswick, 1862

By 1862, sixteen-year-old Mary Corbett had been in service to the Skerrett family of Ullingswick for about eighteen months. She was variously described as 'a good, steady little girl' and as a 'strong, ruddy and good-looking girl', who was always cheerful and a willing worker.

On 20 October 1862, Elizabeth Skerrett sent Mary on an errand to the local beer house, the Drainer's Arms, which also incorporated a small shop. Asked to purchase beer, candles and pins, Mary returned without the candles and was sent back to fetch them. The shop was only 300 or 400 yards from the Skerrett's home and Mary should have returned within fifteen minutes. When she didn't come back, Mrs Skerrett retraced her route but was unable to find any sign of her maid, who had picked up the forgotten candles and then apparently vanished on her short journey home.

It was a very wet and windy night and the Skerrett family sat up until after three o'clock the following morning, waiting for Mary to come back. Several times Elizabeth or her son, Herbert, went out to look for her, each time returning alone. Eventually, the Skerretts concluded that Mary must have gone off to visit her grandmother and retired to bed, expecting her to return later that morning.

Mary Corbett never came home again. Thatcher William Weaver was staying overnight in the village, at the home of George Hope. At seven o'clock on the morning of 21 October, Weaver went out into the back garden of Hope's cottage and spotted a bundle propped against an apple tree in the orchard behind the cottage. He called Hope and together the two men walked over to the tree to investigate.

The bundle was the body of Mary Corbett, which had been partially covered with a dirty shawl. The young girl was filthy, looking as though she had been rolled in a mixture of blood and thick mud. Her clothes were disarranged, her mouth was filled with congealed blood and her hair hung in matted strands around her face. Hope prodded her gently with his toe, finding her body to be completely stiff. The two men realised instantly that the girl had been brutally murdered and quickly moved away to avoid disturbing the ground around her, which bore several visible footprints.

Once the police arrived, Mary Corbett's body was placed on a cart and driven to the Prince of Wales Inn in the village, where it was undressed and washed prior to a post-mortem examination being carried out by surgeons Mr Henry Graves Bull of Hereford and Mr Hill of Bodenham. The doctors determined that death had occurred as a result of asphyxia or suffocation, due to the compression of her nose, mouth and throat, around which were numerous clearly identifiable fingernail impressions. It seemed as though Mary's attacker had prevented her from breathing by pressure from his hands. He had also violently raped her and the weight of his body on hers had forced the contents of her stomach into her windpipe, causing her to choke on her own vomit.

An examination of the field in which the body was found showed several distinct indentations in the soft earth. There was an unmistakeable depression in the ground where Mary had been lying, her body having sunk into the ground as though pinned down by a great weight on top of it. Where her feet had been positioned were two marks made by the toes of a man's boots and between her legs were several impressions of what looked like corduroy. It didn't take too much imagination to picture Mary lying on her back, with a man lying on top of her, his weight crushing her as he raped her, his hand pressed tightly over her mouth to stifle her screams of pain and terror.

Having searched the immediate area, the police found two more clues. The first was an area of flattened vegetation at the side of the road between the pub and the Skerretts' home, where it seemed a struggle or scuffle had occurred. A woman's hairnet, later identified as belonging to Mary, lay on the verge there. The second clue was a frail – a type of rush basket, in this case filled with turnips – which was found in a corner of the orchard.

The frail was quite distinctive, having several pieces of cord attached to it and several people who saw it suggested that it might belong to William Hope, the brother of George, one of the two men who had found the body. William was a known criminal who, in 1850, had been sentenced to seven years transportation. He had returned to Ullingswick after just three years on a ticket of leave, since when he had committed a number of petty crimes, some of which had earned him a short prison sentence.

Interviewing William Hope became a priority for the police and PC Thomas Simpson was despatched to track him down. He found him in a pear tree, where he was busy shaking down pears for a local farmer, Mr Wood. Simpson arrested William on suspicion of the murder of Mary Corbett, at which William went deathly pale. Simpson cautioned him that anything he said might be used against him. 'I shall say nothing,' said William determinedly and he was as good as his word.

An inquest was opened at the Prince of Wales Inn by coroner Mr Lanwarne, at which William Hope's movements on the night of the murder were detailed. Mary Bevan, the proprietor of the shop and beer house, told the inquest that, in order to get to the shop, Mary would have passed through the beer house kitchen. Mrs Bevan recalled that although 'there was a good drop of drink stirring' that night, when Mary arrived for the second time only two customers remained in the kitchen – John Prosser, who was intoxicated and had fallen asleep, and William Hope. On Mary's first visit, Hope had tried to persuade her to drink some beer with him but she had politely refused. When Mary came back for the candles at about 9.50 p.m., Hope had tried once more to get her to have a drink, even going as far as to order a glass of beer for her.

Mary had refused again and left to return home. Almost as soon as she walked out of the beer house door, Hope stood up and followed her, leaving behind almost a quart of beer in the jug on the table.

Herbert Skerrett had briefly visited the Drainer's Arms that evening to buy beer to take home with him. After leaving for home, he had met with Mary Corbett as she walked to the beer house for her second visit of the night. Herbert stated that he had seen a frail of turnips outside the beer house as he entered and left the premises. Both Herbert and Mary Bevan told the coroner that, on previous occasions, Mary had accepted a drink from William Hope and neither had ever seen him attempting to 'take liberties' with her.

Richard Mapp lived roughly halfway between the beer house and the Skerretts' home. He told the inquest that he had heard two short screams at around ten o'clock at night, which he believed came from the spot on the roadside where there was evidence of a scuffle. Mapp had opened his bedroom window and listened intently for a while but the wind was very blustery and he had heard nothing further. Mapp described the screams as sounding like a woman in distress.

William Weaver and George Hope described finding the body, with George stating that the frail was very similar in appearance to one owned by his brother.

William Hope's landlady, Sarah Prosser, told the inquest that William had not come home on the evening of 20 October. He had been lodging with her for roughly four weeks by then and was well aware of the house rule – if lodgers weren't indoors by ten o'clock at night, the doors were locked and they were refused admittance. Sarah had not gone to bed herself until about half-past eleven on the night of the murder, at which time there had been no sign of William. It was the first time he had ever been locked out for being too late home.

Several people stated that William Hope had been wearing a dark-coloured or black coat when he left the beer house yet, when he was arrested the next morning, the garment was nowhere to be found. One of the villagers, James Weaver, took it upon himself to go and search for the missing coat, which he eventually found rolled up and concealed in a hollow tree in a coppice, roughly 150 yards from the roadside where the initial struggle had occurred. Weaver then handed the coat to PC Simpson.

Simpson recounted the arrest of William Hope and said that he had escorted him to the Prince of Wales Inn, where he had shown him the frail and asked Hope if it belonged to him. 'I suppose it must do,' replied Hope, who was then taken to the police station at Bromyard.

There his clothing was examined by Superintendent Daniel Harwood and compared with the marks found in the mud by Mary Corbett's body. Hope's twill trousers had exactly the same appearance as the imprints of the ridges in the dirt. The knees of his trousers were dirty, as were his shirt cuffs and his billycock hat and there were spots of blood on those garments, as well as on a smock that he had been wearing over his shirt. Most tellingly, there were also spots of blood on his underclothes and on the inside of the buttoned flap at the front of his trousers. When the coat found in the hollow tree was later handed in to the police, it also bore spots of blood and Mrs Bevan subsequently positively identified it as the coat worn by William Hope on the night of the murder, saying that she remembered a distinctive rent near the left-hand pocket.

After hearing evidence for six hours, the coroner's jury felt no need to debate their verdict and William Hope was committed by coroner's warrant to stand trial at the next Hereford Assizes on a charge of 'wilful murder'. He was taken to Hereford Gaol, having kept to his resolution to say nothing throughout the inquest.

Hope's trial opened at Hereford on 27 March 1863 before Mr Baron Channell. Mr W.H. Cooke and Mr Cleave appeared for the prosecution, while Mr H. James acted for the defence. Hope, who pleaded 'Not Guilty', was described in the newspapers of the time as a 'stout, thick-necked, burly-looking fellow, whose physiognomy tends to a low estimate of his moral character.'

Much of the evidence heard in court was a repeat of that presented at the inquest, although there was one further piece of damning evidence against William Hope. Mr Bull, who had performed the post-mortem examination on Mary Corbett, also served as the medical officer at the Hereford County Gaol, where Hope had been incarcerated since the murder, awaiting his trial. Having given his evidence about his findings on examining the victim, Bull went on to say that, on 27 October, he had also treated William Hope in prison.

Mr Justice Channell, 1897. (Author's collection)

Hope had been suffering from a 'gathering' on the second joint of the middle finger of his left hand. The pus-filled infection was causing him great pain and, when Bull examined Hope's hand, he noted the presence of six recent scabs. Bull stated that, in his opinion, the injuries to Hope's hand were consistent with a human bite and that they were about a week old.

In defence of William Hope, Mr James indicated that his client's innocence had been satisfactorily proved by the evidence presented in court. He drew particular attention to the testimony of Mrs Bevan, the landlady of the Drainer's Arms.

Mrs Bevan had seemed slightly confused by the timing of events on the night of the murder and, when pressed to be more accurate had responded, 'My head is so bad I cannot answer.' Nevertheless, she had clearly described watching Mary Corbett leaving the inn for the second time on the night of her murder, repeatedly saying that Mary had run away towards home. Mrs Bevan described Mary's gait as 'a bit of a run homewards', adding, 'As long as I watched Mary Corbett down the road she continued on the run.' Mrs Bevan had then stated that William Hope had not left the pub for at least two minutes after Mary's departure.

Given that William Hope was laden with a heavy basket of turnips, how could he possibly have overtaken Mary, who had a two minute head start on him and was running home rather than walking, asked the counsel for the defence?

Hope had stated that, on the night of the murder, he had been too late to return to his lodgings and so had slept in Mrs Bevan's stable. Although nobody had seen him there either that night or on the following morning, Mrs Bevan testified that he had slept in her stable before and that she had once found him lying in the manger at six o'clock in the morning.

Mr James pointed out that Hope had made no attempt to avoid capture and had made no effort to clean the mud and blood from his clothing. Shortly before the murder, he was known to have worked on a very muddy job, cleaning out a brook for a farmer – his clothes could have got dirty then and the blood spots on them could easily have come from the injury to his own hand, observed by Mr Bull.

Once the judge had summed up the evidence, the jury retired for thirty minutes before returning with a 'Guilty' verdict. William Hope showed not the slightest sign of emotion as he listened to the judge pronouncing the death sentence.

His sullen and morose attitude continued as he awaited his execution in the condemned cell at Hereford Gaol. However, as his final day neared, he began to show some penitence and to look to the religious ministrations of the prison chaplain for comfort. He finally confessed to the rape and murder of young Mary Corbett on the eve of his execution, which took place before a large crowd of people on 15 April 1863. Unlike his victim, thirty-year-old William Hope was reported by the contemporary newspapers to have 'died easily'.

11

'A MAN IS A VILLAIN WHO TAKES AN AXE TO A WOMAN'

Hennor, near Leominster, 1864

Thomas Watkins of Hennor, near Leominster, could best be described as an idle layabout, who refused point blank to get a job and support his wife and family. As well as bringing up two young children with precious little help from her husband, Mary Ann Watkins was forced to earn sufficient money to feed and clothe them and keep a roof over their heads, which she did by working as a charwoman and taking in washing. She was also allowed a small amount of parish relief.

Mary Ann was a very pretty woman and, as a young girl, had been seduced by a person of a much higher social status, an affair that ended in what the contemporary newspapers described as 'her ruin and disgrace'. When she married Thomas, he never allowed her to forget her status as a fallen woman and throughout their marriage he continually accused her of being unfaithful to him, something which she denied over and over again. Thomas was an exceptionally jealous husband and, in November 1863, two men who he believed Mary Ann to be attracted to were found dead in the River Lugg, in highly suspicious circumstances.

In 1861, Thomas Watkins enlisted in the Royal Marines, although his long-suffering wife and children saw vey little of his pay. However, the strict military regimes didn't suit him and he soon deserted, returning to the Leominster area. There he alternated living with his wife at her lodgings with sleeping rough in barns and farm outbuildings.

The Board of Guardians administered the payment of funds and the supply of extra food to the poor of the parish and as soon as they discovered that Watkins

Hennor. (© R. Sly)

had returned to the area, they set about trying to make him take care of his responsibilities. As an initial step, Mary Ann was summoned to appear before the Board to explain her financial circumstances, which she did on 5 January 1864. At that meeting, a further appointment was arranged for 19 January and Mary Ann was told that although her payments from the parish would continue until that date, from then on her husband would be expected to contribute to her upkeep.

When Thomas Watkins got wind of his wife's appearance before the Board of Guardians, he was furious. On 14 January, he spoke to Mrs Rebecca Martin, telling her that Mary Ann had been to the gentlemen of the Board and said everything in her power against him. Watkins bemoaned the fact that Mary Ann had another appointment with the board in five days time, saying that he knew that she would have more to say. He swore an oath that she would never have the chance to say anything against him again. Unfortunately, Mrs Martin didn't take his threats seriously and neither did those who observed him patrolling the area around Hennor two days before his wife's scheduled meeting, carrying a large, stout stick, which he referred to as his 'keep-safe'.

On 18 January, Mary Ann Watkins went to work at the home of gardener Mr Lane, who lived about a mile from her lodgings. Having spent the day doing Lane's laundry, she left for home in the early evening, carrying a packet of dripping that she had been given for the children.

Her route took her through several fields and had been walked just minutes earlier by Mr Lane as he returned home. Lane was accompanied by his dog and, at one stage, the dog suddenly stopped dead, raised its hackles and began to growl. Mr Lane could see nothing out of the ordinary that might have caught the dog's attention, so simply called the animal to heel and continued home.

Some four hours later, a Mr Lipscombe was walking the same footpath when he heard a low moaning noise. He followed the sound to the corner of a ploughed field, where he found a woman lying face down on the ground in a pool of blood.

Lipscombe rushed to the nearest house, which was Mr Lane's cottage and, having collected a lantern, the two men went to see if they could assist the woman. Mr Lane immediately recognised her as Mary Ann Watkins and together the men carried her to her lodgings in Hennor. Lane then borrowed a horse and cart, on which he took the injured woman to Leominster workhouse, where she died the following afternoon without regaining consciousness. A post-mortem examination revealed that she had several large bruises on her body, as though she had been severely beaten. An onslaught of blows had apparently forced her to her knees, at which whoever had attacked her had hit her hard on the back of the head with a blunt instrument, causing a fractured skull and terrible damage to her brain.

When the police examined the field where Mary Ann was found in daylight on the following morning, they noticed an abundance of fresh footprints, which appeared to have been made by wooden-soled boots or clogs. The shape of the footwear that had produced the impressions in the soft earth was quite distinctive, since the toes were very pointed and there appeared to be a thin band of metal running around the rim of the soles. While one officer was detailed to take wax and plaster casts of the prints, assisted by Leominster chemist and druggist Mr Giles, eight constables were sent to check nearby farm buildings and two superintendents set out to try and follow the trail of footprints, in the hope that it would eventually lead them to Mary Ann's attacker.

The prints led back towards Mary Ann's lodgings, passing the house where she lived before continuing on towards the village of Stretford. There it was found that a man had called on a Mrs Jones at about 9.45 p.m. on the previous evening, asking for some tobacco and a bed for the night. Mrs Jones and her son told police that the man had seemed very nervous and highly agitated, so much so that he had made them feel uncomfortable and they had quickly sent him on his way. According to Mrs Jones, the man told her, 'I am very uneasy in my mind. I have a very good mind to drown myself before morning.'

The footprints then led towards the Trumpet Inn, following the Leominster to Bromyard road, before doubling back. The officers lost the trail but managed to find it again about a quarter of a mile further down the road towards Bromyard.

Whoever had made the prints seemed to have no clear idea where he or she was heading, since the trail led back and forth through gates and in and out of fields seemingly at random, often doubling back on itself. The officers followed the trail as far as Risbury before losing it again near the home of Mr John Pritchard. This was very close to the home of Thomas Watkins' mother, although she was away at the time, nursing her sick daughter at Ladycott. Nevertheless, a watch was placed on her house and the outbuildings were thoroughly searched. By then, darkness was falling and the two officers retired to the Maidenhead Inn at Pencumbe for the night. To their surprise, in the light of the following day, they could clearly see the footprints in the area around the pub.

The tracks curved around for some seven miles, although, as the crow flies, they covered only roughly a three-mile distance. By nightfall, the trackers were heading towards Brierly.

The following morning, the police picked up the trail again, searching outbuildings and talking to householders on their way. They were told that a stranger had been seen wandering in a place called Quarry Hole, from where his tracks led to a cottage, where the man had begged for food. Given some bread by the lady of the house, he told her, 'This is the first time I have broken my fast this day.'

The tracks led onwards through Brierly Woods to Ivington Camp, where they disappeared temporarily before resuming two fields later. The prints took the police officers to Ivington Court, where they learned that a man had asked for a drink at six o'clock on the previous evening. He had left after having drunk a pint of cider but fortunately someone had seen him leaving and was able to show the police in which direction he had gone.

Now the trail led across several fields to Wintercott and from there to Horden. However, once the prints reached Horden, the officers realised that they had made a mistake and were following a different set of prints. They retraced their steps back to Wintercott and from there continued on a zig-zag course to the Kington–Leominster turnpike road, where the man had apparently stopped at a cottage to ask for a light for his pipe.

On went the footprints and on went the police in pursuit of their quarry. Finally, as they approached Mr Bray's house near Eardisland, the police saw a man on the doorstep, talking to Mrs Bray. 'It's you, Watkins,' exclaimed Superintendent Dyke, as he got close enough to recognise the man. Watkins didn't deny his identity, standing quietly as Superintendent Alexander handcuffed him. When he was charged with murdering his wife, Watkins did not reply but later, as he was being escorted back to Leominster police station, he stated, 'It was not me that done it; you may take me for desertion and that's all.'

By the time his case was brought before magistrates, Thomas Watkins had changed his mind and was cheerfully pleading 'Guilty' to the wilful murder of his wife. Committed to appear at the next Assizes, his trial opened in Hereford on 24 March 1864, before Mr Baron Pigott, and, once again, Watkins pleaded 'Guilty' to the charge against him.

Pigott asked if he would rather have the case against him legally proved or if he wished to persevere with his guilty plea. Watkins said that he didn't much care, since he was guilty anyway, but agreed to do whatever the judge thought best. Pigott directed the clerk of the court to record a plea of 'Not Guilty' then asked Watkins if he had an attorney or counsel.

Watkins admitted that he didn't, at which Mr Weightman stepped forward and informed the judge that the defendant's mother had spoken to him about defending her son and that, even now, there was an attorney with Watkins' mother, awaiting instructions.

Pigott asked Watkins if he wished his mother to arrange legal assistance for him and Watkins replied that he did not. Pigott decided that Watkins' mother had no legal right to insist that her son was defended, if that was against the defendant's wishes. He then turned to Watkins and asked if he wanted him to arrange a counsel for him.

Watkins told the judge to do whatever pleased him, as he was guilty, although he was eventually to accept his mother's offer of assistance and, with the defendant now properly represented, the trial could proceed.

In the face of such indifference from his client, the counsel for the defence had an uphill struggle ahead of him. He tried valiantly to put forward an argument for the reduction of the charge against Watkins from murder to manslaughter, on the grounds that Watkins had been provoked into killing his wife. However, the prosecution had already produced a string of witnesses to whom Watkins had spoken on his half-hearted cross country flight from justice, including a Mrs Nash, at whose home Watkins had stopped to ask for a light for his pipe.

Not surprisingly, the conversation had turned to the gruesome murder that was by then the talk of the entire area. 'A man is a villain who takes an axe to a woman,' Mrs Nash had commented, doubtless unaware that she was actually confronting that villain on her own doorstep at that very moment.

'It was not an axe, it was a stake,' Watkins corrected her.

In his summary of the case for the jury, Pigott told them that there was nothing whatsoever in the evidence to support the defence counsel's argument that Watkins had been provoked in any way and neither had anyone come forward to suggest that Mary Ann Watkins had ever provoked her husband. Therefore, if the jury believed the evidence, then the charge could be nothing short of murder and the only question they needed to consider was whether or not the defendant was the man who committed the crime.

The jury were quick to return a verdict of 'Guilty' and Thomas Watkins listened disinterestedly as a sentence of death was passed upon him.

From the condemned cell at Hereford Gaol, Watkins was to make a full confession to the murder of his wife to the prison governor and chaplain, although he categorically denied any involvement in the suspicious deaths of the two men found in the River Lugg. Watkins stated that he believed that Mary Ann was going to give him up to the Board of Poor-Law Guardians and had killed her to prevent her from doing so. Although he continued to insist that his wife had provoked him, he now appeared to deeply regret her murder and seemed genuinely sorry for his actions.

On 5 April 1864, Watkins walked to the scaffold with a firm, unfaltering step to meet executioner George Smith. It was a very wet morning and the crowd of spectators who had gathered to watch the execution was considerably smaller than was usual on such occasions. It was to be the last ever public execution at Hereford Gaol.

12

'... TROUBLE, PERPLEXITY AND NO SMALL EXPENSE'

Dinmore Wood, 1878

In the nineteenth century, Dinmore Wood was a popular Herefordshire beauty spot and, on Easter Monday in April 1878, a large picnic party was organised there. Little did the picnickers know that, within a few yards of their merriment, a woman's body lay in the undergrowth waiting to be discovered.

The remains were finally found on 23 May and were so badly decomposed that identification initially proved impossible. The woman's face had been almost completely eaten away by insects and her brain was missing. Animals had feasted on her limbs and had taken large pieces of flesh, particularly from her left leg, which had been almost totally consumed, presumably by either dogs or foxes.

The police were called to the site of the gruesome discovery and Superintendent Dykes, one of the first officers to arrive on the scene, noticed a quantity of dried greenish substance on the forest floor, close to the woman's head. There was similar matter caked around the remains of the woman's mouth, leading the Superintendent to believe that it was either vomit or some other form of discharge. It appeared as if some sort of struggle had taken place in the immediate area and there were scuff marks on the ground which seemed to indicate that the dead woman had been dragged a short distance to her final resting place, which was about 100 yards from the nearest road.

The woman was about 5ft 3in tall, well-nourished and wearing a black silk skirt and a cloth jacket trimmed with black silk and bearing distinctive metal buttons. In addition, she wore a very fashionable hat, trimmed with blue velvet and red feathers. Her undergarments were of the finest quality and included a hand-tailored scarlet cashmere petticoat and what the police termed as 'fancy garters', which were lined with red cloth. Concealed in her clothing was a small leather purse, which contained a single penny, and there were numerous tiny fragments of paper scattered around the body.

Such was the condition of the woman's remains that the police were unable to estimate her age beyond saying that she was probably between twenty-five and forty years old. What was perhaps most surprising was that there had been no reports of any missing women in the area.

A post-mortem examination was carried out on the remains by Dr Mason, who estimated that the woman had been dead for at least a month and most probably much longer. The body was so decomposed that Mason struggled to draw any firm conclusions about how she had died. However, he was able to state with certainty that there were two fractures in the woman's skull, the first of which was about one inch long and the second almost three and a half inches in length. In Mason's opinion, the fractures were marks of violence, resulting from two heavy blows that had been inflicted before her death. Given the condition of the body and in the absence of the woman's brain, he was unable to state definitively that the wounds to her head had been the cause of her death. Neither was he able to determine conclusively whether or not the woman had been raped or sexually assaulted, although most of the newspapers of the time reported that she had been 'violated' before her death and intimated that there were unmistakeable signs that a 'double crime' had been committed on the unfortunate woman.

Establishing the woman's identity became a priority for the police. Her clothes appeared to be stained with what looked like drops of blood and were sent to public analyst Dr Horsley from Cheltenham, to see if he could determine exactly what the stains were. However, having been exposed to the elements for so long, the stains on the garments proved impossible to classify.

The first apparent break in the case came from witnesses who told police that they had heard cries of 'Murder!' coming from within the wood on the night after a National Hunt horse racing event at Hereford racecourse, which was situated approximately seven miles to the south. It was suggested that the body might be that of an itinerant musician who had attended the race meeting and had afterwards been seen arguing with her husband. The police went to great lengths to try and trace the nameless musician, who was eventually found alive and well at Gloucester.

The police then heard rumours that William Smith, the landlord of the Kerry Arms Hotel in Hereford, suspected that the dead woman was one of his guests who had vanished without trace in February. Both Smith and his wife, Sarah, had been freely discussing their suspicions since the discovery of the body and had even written letters to family members saying that they believed that the unidentified body in the wood was that of a long-term resident of the hotel who had disappeared, owing them a considerable amount of money. Amazingly, they had not thought to mention their concerns to the police and, even when they were interviewed, they seemed reluctant to get involved and loath to impart any information willingly. Indeed, a report in the *Illustrated Police News* bemoans the '...trouble, perplexity and no small expense' caused to the police by their reticence and states: 'They volunteered nothing whatever; the police had to positively drag the information out of them.' (William Smith was later to explain that he and his wife had heard that the woman had been identified as a servant girl and had thought that they had been mistaken in assuming that she was their missing guest.)

William and Sarah Smith eventually told the police that they believed that the dead woman was Miss Jane Hannah Jay. Miss Jay was a regular guest at the hotel, frequently staying there for periods of two or three months. Most recently, she had been a guest of the hotel from November 1877 until her unexplained disappearance in February 1878.

During her latest stay at the hotel, she had made no attempt to pay her bill. The hotel was on the verge of a change in ownership and therefore, on 10 February 1878, Mrs Smith presented her with an invoice for the outstanding amount of £22 16s. 'I know you want your money, don't you?' Miss Jay said, before telling Mrs Smith that she didn't have sufficient funds to settle her account. However, she assured Mrs Smith that she would obtain some money from her friends and left the hotel on the afternoon of 19 February, promising to return in three days time.

The Kerry Hotel (formerly the Kerry Arms Hotel). (© N. Sly)

Mrs Smith told the police that, during her stay, Miss Jay had often left the hotel for short periods and that she had no reason to suspect that she wouldn't return with the money as promised. When Miss Jay failed to come back to the hotel, the contents of her room were boxed and put into storage. When the police examined the boxes, they found a number of metal buttons that exactly matched those on the dead woman's jacket.

The dead woman's clothes were taken to the hotel where they were positively identified as belonging to Miss Jay by both Mrs Smith and her niece, Emily. Furthermore when the fragments of paper found scattered around the body were pieced together, they were found to be the hotel bill given to Miss Jay shortly before her disappearance.

The police went to visit Miss Jay's family and learned from her brother, Edward, that in September 1877 he had paid her the sum of £14 8s in settlement of a personal debt. Jane had then gone to Hereford and rented a house in Commercial Street, in which she intended to open a shop. She had partially furnished the house and had put a few things in the shop window but had never moved into the premises.

Edward Jay travelled to Hereford, bringing with him Mrs Sarah Dingley, a farmer's wife from Little Hereford. Mrs Dingley examined the clothes worn by the dead woman and told police that they were very similar to those owned by Jane Jay. When it came to the red petticoat, she was even more positive that the garment belonged to Jane, since she had made it for her herself. She pointed out to the police a small area of the herring bone stitching where she had accidentally made a mistake, saying that it was such a tiny error that she hadn't thought it worth the bother of rectifying.

An inquest had already been opened by coroner Mr Henry Moore and adjourned to allow the police more time to establish the identity of the woman. Once the inquest was resumed, Edward Jay and the hotel staff gave evidence of Miss Jay's character.

Jane Jay, who was actually thirty-two years old, was described as suffering from 'frequent fits of melancholy' which, coupled with occasional 'eccentric behaviours', caused those who knew her to '...regard her with some misgivings as to her complete sanity' although, as the newspapers were quick to point out, 'her demeanour on the whole does not appear to have caused any special anxiety or any doubts as to her ability to take care of herself.'

Miss Jay had left a number of pieces of jewellery in her hotel room, including some that were quite valuable. Yet she never seemed to have any money and, on occasions, was forced to borrow a penny from the staff to post a letter. While resident at the hotel, she kept herself to herself and avoided any communication with the hotel staff unless it was absolutely necessary. Occasionally she was absent from the hotel all night, often returning in the morning very wet and bedraggled, having apparently walked for some distance. She was very much a loner, although Mrs Smith told the inquest that she had occasionally received visits from a gentleman. She had also once told Mrs Smith that she was married and that her real name was 'Mrs Bevis', receiving several letters at the hotel addressed to her in that name. Superintendent Cope stated that, having made every possible enquiry, he had been unable to find any evidence that Miss Jay had ever married.

Jane Reed, a servant at the hotel, said that Miss Jay was often very strange in her ways and, on one occasion, had told her that she thought that she should go away and leave all her clothes and jewellery for Mrs Smith, in settlement of her bill.

Edward Jay told the inquest that he believed his sister might once have been disappointed in love and that, as a result, she had expressed a desire to kill herself. Nine years earlier she had been 'a little flighty', but she had always been rational.

The police had surmised that, on leaving the hotel, it had been Miss Jay's intention to walk to her home in Kimbolton to obtain some money. Mrs Smith believed that she was intending to be away for three days and the police theorised that she had allowed herself one day to walk home, followed by a day of rest, before returning to the hotel.

When Miss Jay left the hotel at between two and three o'clock on the afternoon of 19 February, the landlord's son, Thomas, was told to watch her in order to make sure that she wasn't heading for the station, intending to leave without paying her bill. Thomas followed Miss Jay outside and watched her turn into Widemarsh Street. Satisfied that she was heading towards her home at Stockton Court, Kimbolton, rather than to the station, he did not follow her any farther. At half-past six that evening, carpenter George Griffiths, who knew Jane Jay well, saw her walking close to the spot where her body was later found.

Everyone was at a loss to explain how and why Jane Jay had met her death. Given that she was known to be depressed and had possibly even entertained thoughts of ending her own life, suicide seemed a likely possibility. It was easy, said the coroner, to imagine that her mind had become unhinged and that the large hotel bill, which she had no ready means of paying, had driven her to despair. However, the theory of suicide did not fit with the two head wounds observed by Dr Mason.

Mason had in fact performed a second post-mortem examination on the body of Jane Jay, and another doctor, Dr John Elliott, had also examined the body, although Mason's investigations had by then largely destroyed what little was left of it, making it difficult for Elliott to draw any firm conclusions. Mason was called before the coroner to outline his findings for the inquest jury.

He reiterated finding two large fractures in Miss Jay's skull, one of which was on the very top of her head and the other on the parietal bone at the side of her head, towards the top. Mason thought it highly unlikely that these injuries had been caused by a fall, unless Miss Jay had fallen from a great height.

Access to the place where Miss Jay's body was found was difficult and the ground was uneven and slippery. Could Miss Jay have stumbled or slipped and fallen over, hitting her head on a rock or a tree stump, asked the coroner? Mason felt this explanation equally improbable, since there were two wounds and both were located on or towards the top of her head. How could two wounds be the result of one fall? Was it then possible that Miss Jay had simply died from exhaustion, hunger or exposure to the cold? Both doctors felt that this was highly unlikely and didn't explain her head injuries.

With that, the inquest jury retired and, after deliberating for about twenty minutes returned with their verdict. They were satisfied that the deceased woman was Jane Hannah Jay and that she was found dead in Dinmore Wood. How she came by her death there was no evidence to show.

In spite of this verdict, the police were still treating Jane Jay's death as suspicious and had already made an arrest in connection with her supposed murder. Farm labourer James Stringer was apprehended in a public house in Kidderminster after he 'incautiously let fall an expression or two' that suggested he knew far more about the death of Miss Jay than had been published in the newspapers. His remarks were overheard by a clergyman, who reported them to the police.

Stringer was taken to Hereford for questioning but turned out to be the type of man who constantly strived to be the centre of attention. Drink had loosened his tongue and, when the conversation turned to the 'Dinmore mystery', he had been unable to resist bragging about his knowledge of Miss Jay's death. It quickly became evident that he was innocent of her murder, although the police were delighted to find that there was a warrant out for his arrest on an unrelated assault, for which he had already been sentenced in his absence to two months' imprisonment. He was sent to Hereford Gaol to serve his sentence, where he no doubt had more than enough time to rue his unguarded remarks.

A path in Dinmore Wood. (Author's collection)

Thus, the mysterious death of Jane Jay has never been solved. Was it a case of suicide, accident or natural death? Or, as the police and doctors strongly believed at the time, was she murdered? It is worth mentioning that ten years earlier, in October 1868, the body of a twenty-year-old servant, Elizabeth Chandler, was found in almost identical circumstances in a wood near Ludlow, in Shropshire. Like Jane Jay, Lizzie set out to walk home and, two months later, her badly decomposed body was found with head injuries. Nobody had noticed her disappearance as the family she worked for were about to move to America. They thought that she had returned home, while her parents believed that she had gone abroad with her employers. Sunny Dingle, the wood where Lizzie's body was found, was less than fifteen miles from the place where Jane Jay met her untimely death.

Note: The Kerry Arms Hotel has since been renamed The Kerry. There are some minor discrepancies in the contemporary newspaper reports of the murder. The policeman who first examined the body is referred to as both Superintendent Dukes and Superintendent Dykes and, in an earlier chapter of this book, Superintendent Dyke. The wood where the body was found is mostly referred to as Dinmore Wood but, on occasions, is alternatively named as both Dinmow Wood and Queen's Wood.

13

'THIS IS NOT MY ROAD HOME'

Hereford, 1880

James Williams, a native of Abergavenny, worked in Hereford for builder Mr Bowers and lodged with Mr and Mrs Hall in Bewell Street. Fifty-year-old Williams was a sober and respectable man, although according to his landlady, Charlotte Hall, he did enjoy a drink on Saturday nights. Even then, he was usually home by eleven o'clock at the latest but on Saturday, 10 January 1880, he didn't come home at all.

Williams was paid his wages of 30s earlier that day and, as soon as he received his money, he went back to his lodgings to pay his rent. Once he had taken care of his responsibilities, he set off for his normal Saturday night drink but, the following morning, his body was found by boatman Harry Jordan, floating in the River Wye. The water where he was found was less than 3ft deep.

Surgeon Mr A. Skipton was summoned to the scene, where he made an external examination of Williams' body. Skipton found two small abrasions on Williams' fingers and another on his elbow. He came to the conclusion that Williams had drowned, although he noted that the veins in Williams' neck seemed very swollen and there were faint marks on his throat, as if an attempt had been made to strangle him.

When the police checked the contents of Williams' pockets, it was obvious that he had been robbed. Having so recently been paid, he should have had money on his person and his silver watch and chain, pipe and carpenter's rule were also missing, as was the joint of pork that he had bought that afternoon. The river bank where Williams had entered the water bore numerous different footprints and signs that a scuffle had taken place.

The police began to check on Williams' movements during his last hours alive and found that he had been drinking in the Red Lion public house until closing time at eleven o'clock. Williams had three drinking companions – cheese dealer James Davis, usually known as 'Jemmy the Cheese', fitter Andrew Heggie and William Watkins (aka Morris), who was a Private on furlough from the 24th Foot Regiment.

Throughout the night, Williams had been spending his wages freely, paying for drinks for his companions as well as for other drinkers in the pub. By eleven o'clock, he was very drunk and Davis, Heggie and Watkins had volunteered to see him home safely. However several witnesses believed that, rather than seeing him home, the three men forced Williams in a completely different direction, taking him towards the river, where he was later found dead.

At the inquest into Williams' death, all three men appeared before the coroner and, although all three admitted drinking with him, they all strenuously denied any contact with the deceased after the pub closed. As one, they stated that they believed that he had headed off alone down Victoria Street, with a number of people following him, although they were unable to name any of those people.

The coroner concluded that, although there was clear evidence to show that Williams had been attacked and robbed, there was nothing to suggest that he had then been pushed into the water. The coroner's jury returned a verdict of 'found drowned' and the inquest was duly closed, on the understanding that the police would continue to investigate the suspicious death and the inquest would be re-opened if they found any further evidence.

As the investigations progressed, several witnesses came forward to say that they had heard cries of 'Murder!' and the sounds of a fight at about half-past eleven on the night of 10 January, coming from the water meadows where Williams' body was later found. One, Henry Price, had even seen three men leaving the area about fifteen minutes after hearing the cries. He was able to identify Davis as one of the men but unable to identify Heggie or Watkins as being the other two. Two more witnesses stated that they had seen three men manhandling Williams towards the water meadows, later identifying these men as Davis, Watkins and Heggie. Davis and Watkins each had a firm grasp of one of Williams' arms, while Heggie was behind him, pushing him along. Both witnesses clearly heard Williams protesting and saying, 'This is not my road home.'

The police arrested and questioned Davis, Heggie and Watkins, who continued to deny having any contact with Williams after he left the pub. However, all three were positively identified by witnesses as the men who had propelled Williams against his will towards the river and his death. Unsure of whether or not they had sufficient evidence to charge their suspects with wilful murder, the police approached the Mayor of Hereford, Owen Fowler, who applied to the Home Office for an order to exhume Williams' body for further medical examination.

Unsurprisingly, since it had not been buried for long, the body was in a remarkably good condition, although it had a light coating of mould and there were numerous 'meat flies' entombed in the coffin. The body was taken to the mortuary at Hereford Gaol, where a post-mortem examination was performed by surgeons Skipton, Moore and Vevers.

The pink marks of violence on Williams' neck, originally observed by Mr Skipton, were still clearly visible but the doctors were able to confirm conclusively that Williams had died from drowning. All of his organs were healthy, which precluded death from any natural causes, such as a heart attack. The only unanswered question was that of how he came to be in the river in the first place and the overwhelming evidence seemed to suggest that he had been deliberately put there.

The police managed to find two witnesses who had seen James Davis after the alleged murder, one of whom, Charles Whitcomb, told them that Davis had sold a silver watch and chain to Richard Johnson, the landlord of the Rummer Inn in Hereford. When Davis was arrested, he did indeed have a silver watch in his possession, which he was trying to sell, but it was not Williams' watch. Davis did however have a large joint of pork in his house, identical to the one that Williams had purchased shortly before his death.

The police looked more closely at Richard Johnson and found that he had recently sold a silver watch for 11s. Johnson denied all knowledge of the transaction but the police were persistent, eventually refusing to leave Johnson's premises until the watch was produced. Johnson finally capitulated, sending his wife to retrieve it from its buyer. It was positively identified as having belonged to Williams. Johnson had apparently bought the watch from James Davis and sold it on and, when he realised that it could implicate him in a suspected murder, had given Davis another watch and told him to pretend to sell it. Then, if the police asked any awkward questions about whether or not he or Davis had ever been in possession of Williams' watch, they could refute the evidence of anyone who said they had by showing them the substitute watch provided by Johnson. (This was later shown to be one of his own watches that had been left to him many years earlier by his father-in-law.)

The case came up before magistrates at The Guildhall in Hereford. Richard Johnson was also charged with the three prisoners as an accessory to the murder, having harboured Davis and Heggie in the knowledge that they had committed a murder and with buying the watch, knowing it to be stolen.

Throughout several hearings at the magistrates' court, Johnson was the only man of the four accused who was defended. His solicitor, Mr Corner, requested bail, saying that Johnson had been a businessman in the area for twenty-six years without stain on his character. The application was refused by the Chief Constable.

The other three defendants were given plenty of opportunity to question the witnesses, although only Davis actually did so, apparently with considerable acumen. He was described as a 'handsome looking fellow', while Heggie and Watkins, who remained silent and sullen throughout, were 'of the most blackguard looking type'. Yet however articulate Davis might have been in his own defence, his fine words did not deter the magistrates from committing all four defendants for trial at the next Assizes.

The trial, which took place over three days, opened before Mr Justice Hawkins at the Worcestershire Assizes, rather than in Hereford. Watkins was defended by Mr Gresham Wells, while Heggie and Davis were undefended. Offered the benefit of counsel by the judge, Davis preferred to defend himself. Heggie accepted and Mr Darling was appointed to defend him, against a prosecution team of Mr Montagu Williams and Mr Cooke.

The prosecution produced a steady stream of witnesses, all of whom had either seen James Williams being physically dragged by the defendants towards the River Wye, where he met his death, or had seen him in the company of the three defendants after leaving the pub. These witnesses included Mr Taylor, the boot boy at the Red Lion and also a police constable, James Morgan, of the City Police Force.

Henry Price and another witness, Benjamin James, who lived close to the river, testified to hearing the sounds of a fight, along with cries of 'Murder!' coming from the water meadows on the night of Williams' death. The prosecution then called Abraham Vernon, a hawker from Gloucestershire, who admitted to having helped Davis spend some of Williams' stolen money and also the proceeds of the sale of the watch.

Vernon had also heard Watkins and Heggie arguing to be given their share of the spoils, telling the court that they had said that they would 'split' or punch Davis in the head if he didn't pay them. Davis cross-examined Vernon at length before, in an effort to reduce the impact of Vernon's evidence, he finally informed the court, 'This witness is one of the biggest housebreakers and biggest rogues you have ever had in this hall. He is also a transport and ought to be along with us in the dock.'

Charles Whitcomb was called to testify about Davis' attempts to sell the watch, admitting to the court that he had previously 'been in some trouble' for theft. Whitcomb stated that he had tried to distance himself from the sale of the watch as, having been convicted several times, he hadn't wanted to get involved with something that he believed was highly suspicious. Whitcomb had also witnessed Johnson's scheme with the second watch.

Once all the witnesses had appeared, the prosecution and defence counsels gave their closing speeches and, as Davis was defending himself, he too was allowed to speak. He addressed the court as eloquently as he had done at the magistrates' court, reiterating that he had no knowledge whatsoever about the death of James Williams and neither did his two co-defendants. Davis freely admitted stealing Williams' watch and selling it but insisted that he was innocent of the charge of murder against him.

Mr Justice Hawkins then took almost three hours to summarise the evidence for the jury, reminding them that the accused were on trial for murder not robbery and this was the only charge that they should be considering at the moment. Hawkins went on to question how Williams had met his death. He had obviously drowned, said the judge, and had marks of violence on his neck, but how had he got into the water in the first place? The jury must therefore first decide whether they believed that Williams had actually been murdered and, if they did, they must determine whether any – or all – of the three defendants were responsible for murdering him.

If the deceased was thrown into the water, with the intention of getting rid of him temporarily, even if the intention had not been murder, the fact that he was thrown into the water recklessly, without any consideration for whether he drowned or not, would constitute murder in the eyes of the law. If, on the other hand, Williams was attacked and robbed and then simply abandoned to his fate and had either stupidly or drunkenly blundered into the river then Hawkins stated that he didn't personally believe that would consitute murder in the eyes of the law, although he added that there were many other people who would argue differently.

Hawkins closed his summary by asking the jury to consider the three defendants separately on the basis of the evidence presented against each one and to give the accused the benefit of any doubts they might have.

The jury retired for almost two hours before returning to acquit all three prisoners. Mr Justice Hawkins seemed clearly taken aback by their verdict but he promptly empanelled a new jury to hear the charges of robbery against Heggie, Davis, Watkins and Richard Johnson. (Since the defendants had been found 'Not Guilty' of murdering James Williams, Johnson could obviously not be tried as an accessory.) Mr Justice Hawkins was not pleased to find several prospective jurors missing from the antechamber and immediately fined them £10 each.

Mr Montagu Williams and Mr Cooke prosecuted the case and all but Richard Johnson were undefended. Mr Lawrence, for Johnson, told the court that when his client initially bought the watch from Davis, he had not been aware that it was stolen. He had panicked when he realised that he might be implicated in a murder as a result of his innocent purchase and had devised the scheme with the replacement watch to protect himself from the consequences.

Davis again spoke in his own defence, telling the jury that he had admitted from the outset that he had stolen Williams' watch. He had always denied being involved in Williams' death and now he and his co-defendants had been acquitted, as he had known they would be all along, since there was no evidence against them. He had told the truth throughout and would continue to do so now – Heggie and Watkins were not involved and Richard Johnson was also perfectly innocent. Davis insisted that he had stolen the watch with two different accomplices, Charles Whitcomb and Abraham Vernon, both of whom had lied under oath.

Once again, Davis' eloquence failed to save him and the jury needed to retire only briefly to determine that all four defendants were guilty as charged.

On hearing the verdict, Mr Justice Hawkins addressed the prisoners. Telling them that they had been found guilty of stealing Williams' watch, he reminded them somewhat incredulously that they had been acquitted of the graver charge of murder. Nobody who had listened to the evidence of the last two and a half days, said the judge, could fail to be convinced that they had hurried and forced a poor old man in the opposite direction to his lodgings to the place where he would ultimately meet his death.

Even though the jury had acquitted them of murder, how Williams came to be in the water defied all explanation. The only inference that could be drawn was that the defendants had hustled him down to the most dangerous place they could select, placing him in great danger and causing him to die, all for the sake of robbing him of his honestly-earned wages and his watch.

THE ILLUSTRATED LONDON NEWS.

REGISTERED AT THE GENERAL POST-OFFICE FOR TRANSMISSION ABROAD.

No. 2802.—VOL. CI.   SATURDAY, DECEMBER 31, 1892.   TWO WHOLE SHEETS } SIXPENCE. BY POST, 6½D.

Photo by Elliott and Fry, Baker Street, W.

THE LATE MR. MONTAGU WILLIAMS.

Mr Montagu Williams QC, as illustrated in the Illustrated London News. *(Author's collection)*

Hawkins flourished a certificate of character that Davis had given him, saying that it proved how worthless such documents were when the subject could stand in the dock without blushing and admit to robbing a man. The judge then sentenced Davis to ten years of penal servitude.

Watkins was only nineteen years old but had already spent five of those years in a reformatory. His sentence was eight years of penal servitude. It was Heggie's first offence but it was a grave one and Hawkins said that he felt that he had a duty to the public to sentence him to five years.

Finally, Hawkins dealt with Johnson, saying that his substitution of the watch showed him to be a very dangerous person. Johnson had asked the judge to be merciful, on account of his wife and family but Hawkins told him that crime usually brought misery to the innocent, as well as punishment to the guilty and if he listened to such appeals then most crime would go unpunished. Johnson's sentence was seven years of penal servitude.

The doctors discovered marks of violence on James Williams' neck and there were clear signs of a desperate struggle having taken place on the riverbank. With numerous eye and ear witnesses, who testified as one under oath that they had seen Williams being forced towards the river and heard his desperate cries of 'Murder!', one can only wonder at the jury who acquitted the three men responsible for his death.

Note: Andrew Heggie is alternatively named Andrew Eggy and Andrew Keggie in some contemporary accounts of the case. He is variously described as being a fitter and as having no occupation. James Davis is alternatively named Davies in some accounts.

14

'I DO NOT LIKE THE LOOK OF THAT MAN'

Weobley, 1885

Thirty-two-year-old Ann Dickson, otherwise known as Ann Dogerty, Ann Dougherty or Ann Cox, was an itinerant worker or 'tramping woman', who moved around the countryside from farm to farm, undertaking seasonal work whenever it was available. On 30 September 1885, she was picking hops for Mr Rogers at Homme Farm, Dilwyn, near Weobley. Rogers was known throughout the area as a good and fair employer and, in addition to their wages, his workers were provided with a barn to sleep in and daily meals.

The weather on 30 September had been atrocious, with torrential rain and gales, which had kept the hop pickers confined indoors. Ann Dickson had absolutely no money and she also had a five-year-old daughter to feed. Having each borrowed a shilling from Mr Rogers in advance of their wages, Ann Dickson and her friend Mary Ann Farrell set out to walk to Weobley to buy provisions. They left Ann's daughter in the care of the other hop pickers but Mary Ann had her four-month-old baby boy in arms, who she carried tightly wrapped in a shawl against the inclement weather.

Ann Dickson was particularly keen to go into Weobley as she was anticipating a visit from her husband, Daniel Cox. Daniel had recently been freed from Worcester Gaol having served a three-week sentence for beating his wife. Nevertheless, Ann had sent him money for the train fare from Worcester and was expecting him to join her at Weobley that evening.

Having bought their groceries, Ann and Mary Ann went into the Red Lion Inn to await the arrival of Daniel Cox. They were soon joined by two more of the hop pickers currently employed at Homme Farm, a man named Mark Hill and another

Woebley, c. 1960. (Author's collection)

man who went by the nickname of 'Blackbird'. As the evening progressed and the drink flowed, Ann Dickson became quite merry and was soon entertaining the pub by singing, albeit rather tipsily.

Two local men had been drinking in the pub for most of the afternoon and decided to join the little party of hop pickers at their table. John Hill (no relation to Mark Hill) was known as 'Sailor Jack' and, as his name implied, he had spent much of his life at sea. John Williams, who was known as 'Irish Jack', worked in Weobley as a painter and glazier and shared a cottage there with his elderly mother.

Hill and Williams both had a reputation locally as aggressive bullies, who were prone to displays of violent behaviour when drunk. Williams was described as 'not a badly disposed fellow' when sober but had actually been imprisoned twice for affray committed under the influence of drink. Yet initially, when they approached the little group, Hill and Williams were charm personified. They joined in the singing and conversation, plied the two women with drinks bought with their own money and even played with Mary Farrell's baby. The only sour note came from Williams' habit of carelessly brandishing his walking stick around as he talked.

The Red Lion, Weobley. (Author's collection)

Weobley, 2009. (The Red Lion is on the left.) (© N. Sly)

It was a stout ash wood stick with a large lump at the top and Mary Farrell was petrified that he would accidentally hit her baby with it. Eventually, she felt obliged to take the stick from him. He surrendered it without protest and, later in the evening, she returned it to him on condition that he would refrain from waving it around.

Towards the end of the evening, Mary Ann began to feel cold and left her seat at the table for one next to the fire. Williams followed her and sat down next to her, cheekily placing his hand on her knee and giving her a friendly squeeze. Mary Ann gave him a black look and pointedly moved to another seat on the other side of the fire. However Williams was not easily deterred and he too moved seats, once again attempting an unwelcome intimacy with Mary Ann.

Mary Ann moved again, this time making sure that there was a table between her and Williams. When Williams moved the table in an effort to get closer to her, Mary Ann went into the pub kitchen to avoid him and stood by herself in the corner.

Meanwhile, his friend John Hill had been attempting similar liberties with Ann Dickson, presumably with slightly more success. At one point during the evening he had left the pub, returning minutes later dressed to impress in his Sunday-best suit.

By half-past nine, when there was still no sign of Daniel Cox, Ann and Mary Ann reluctantly decided that they should return to Homme Farm without him. While they had been enjoying themselves in the pub, the weather had worsened considerably and it was now quite dark. When the women expressed a fear of walking back to the farm in the dark, John Hill gallantly offered to escort them. As the trio left the pub, Mary Ann noticed John Williams standing in a nearby doorway, his stick in his hands. Worried, she pointed him out to Ann, telling her, 'I am going to the police station. I do not like the look of that man,' but Ann was too merry with drink to be concerned and told her friend not to be so soft.

The two women chatted together as they walked back towards the farm, with John Hill trying frequently to interject. Eventually, he made some vulgar suggestions to the women, which they ignored.

After half a mile, the three came to a ploughed field. Mary Ann stepped forward to open the gate and was suddenly and unexpectedly attacked. Something hit her hard on the head, badly injuring her right eye. With blood pouring from her head, Mary Ann slumped to the ground stunned. When she came round it was to find a man lying on top of her, tearing at her clothes and fumbling with her body, with the obvious intention of raping her.

Recognising her assailant as John Williams, Mary Ann fought desperately to escape him. 'If you won't let me quiet, I will kill you,' Williams told her. Twice Mary Ann managed to scramble to her feet, only to be pushed to the ground again. Mary Ann's baby was by now screaming in terror and Williams snatched it from her arms and flung it across the field in temper, threatening again to kill both Mary Ann and the baby if she didn't submit quietly to his demands.

Mary Ann thought very quickly. Telling Williams that the sound of her crying baby might attract the attention of a policeman, she suggested that they would be more comfortable in the barn at Homme Farm and promised William that, if he wanted, he could spend the whole night there with her. Williams fell for her ploy and, after allowing her to pick up her baby he placed his arm around her waist and led her towards the barn. Throughout the walk, Mary Ann forced herself to be compliant and even flirtatious with her attacker. However, as soon as they reached the cottage of Charles Whitefoot, the farm shepherd, she screamed 'Murder!' at the top of her voice and made a desperate run for safety.

Williams promptly fled, leaving Mary Ann shaken and bruised. Such was the force of the attack that one of her teeth had been knocked clean out and others were loose. Blood still streamed from the cut over her eye and her clothes were torn and plastered with mud. Fortunately, the shepherd was at home and came to her aid, escorting her safely back to the barn. There she immediately asked if Ann Dickson had returned and, when she was told that she hadn't, said sadly, 'Then she is murdered.' Mary Ann could not persuade any of the other hop pickers to venture out into the dark, stormy night to help her search for her friend, so spent a sleepless night worrying.

At shortly after six o'clock the following morning, two roadmen, William Jones and Richard Preece, stumbled across the dead body of Ann Dickson propped up against the bank of a pea field, approximately 170 yards from the gate where Mary Ann had first been hit. Ann had obviously been viciously attacked and dreadfully injured. One of her eyes was completely missing and, at a later post-mortem examination, the doctors found that it had been driven into her brain by a heavy blow. The front of her skull was smashed like an eggshell and more than forty splinters of bone had penetrated her brain. There was evidence that a desperate struggle had taken place in several areas near to where Ann's body was discovered and marks on the ground indicated that she had been dragged for some distance to her final resting place. Ann had apparently put up a tremendous fight against her attacker(s) and fragments of human skin were found beneath her fingernails. Her clothing was in disarray, with her dress pulled up around her waist and her stockings down around her ankles.

One of the roadmen stayed with the body while the other ran to Weobley to alert the police. By the time he arrived, Mary Ann Farrell had already walked into the village and told her story to Superintendent Ovens. Ovens went straight to the cottage that John Williams shared with his mother, finding Williams still fast asleep in bed. The clothes that he had been wearing the previous night were scattered around his bedroom and were heavily stained with both mud and blood.

Arrested for the murder of Ann Dickson, Williams appeared surprised and asked Ovens, 'Was that the woman with the baby?' When told that Mary Ann Farrell had been the one with the baby, Williams swore that he had been with Mary Ann rather than the murdered woman. However, he told Ovens that he knew who had struck the blow that killed Ann.

Having apprehended John Williams and locked him up in the police cells, Ovens went in search of John Hill, finding that he had disappeared from his lodgings. Knowing him to be a sailor, Ovens guessed that he would try to board a ship and so telegraphed his description to the nearest ports at Cardiff, Newport and Swansea:

> John Hill, a seaman, native of Weobley but has only just returned from the sea. 32 or 33 years of age, 5'6" high, dark hair, small, light moustache, no beard or whiskers, has a ship tattooed on right arm, nose slightly turned to the side, dressed in dark or black cloth coat, vest and trousers, soft billycock hat turned up at the sides and dented in the top, clean cotton shirt with light brown stripes and elastic sided boots.

By 2 October, John Hill had reached Newport, where he went to the Seamen's Institute and asked for a sheet of paper and an envelope. When they were given to him, he dictated a letter to his brother, Henry, asking him for money to help him escape. Given that his face and hands were badly scratched and his clothes spattered with blood, Hill then stupidly went into the police station at Newport to request a bed ticket for the local workhouse. The officer at the desk had received the telegram from his Herefordshire colleagues and recognised Hill instantly as being their wanted suspect, even though Hill had already given him a false name and address. To confirm his suspicions, he pushed back Hill's coat sleeve, revealing the tattoo of the full-rigged ship on his arm. Realising that he had been identified, Hill immediately turned pale and began to tremble, tears welling up in his eyes and slowly trickling down his cheeks.

Superintendent Ovens went to Newport to collect Hill, travelling by train to Hereford securely handcuffed to his quarry. Even as they arrived at Hereford station the inquest into the death of Ann Dickson was being opened at the workhouse in Weobley by coroner Mr Moore.

Dr William Walker revealed that Ann Dickson had been so badly disfigured by her killer that the only way that her husband Daniel could identify her was by previous surgery to her left breast, part of which had been removed some years earlier. Walker stated that the cause of Ann's death was blows from a blunt instrument that had been so fierce that her skull was shattered and her eye and fragments of bone were forced into her brain. The police had found John Williams' stick at the scene of the crime close to where Ann's body lay. The stick had split and the fist-sized lump of wood at the top had broken off completely. According to Dr Walker, Ann's wounds could have been made with Williams' stick. Dr Walker's painstaking work was later acknowledged in a letter from the Treasury:

> Sir, Re: Hill and Williams. I have to thank you for the able and exhaustive report and analyses you made in this case, which rendered it unnecessary to refer to a medical expert. I have pleasure in enclosing an order for £10 as an addition to the expenses allowed to you by the county.

Williams was present at the inquest and, in the words of the *Hereford Times*, 'maintained an exceedingly indifferent demeanour throughout.' The inquest was adjourned to allow the police time to conclude their enquiries and, by the time it was resumed, both Hill and Williams had already been charged with the murder of Ann Dickson, had appeared before magistrates at Weobley and been committed for trial at the next Gloucester Assizes. Expressing irritation at the fact that the magistrates had pre-empted the inquest, the coroner recorded the verdict of 'wilful murder' against John Williams and John Hill arrived at by the inquest jury.

The trial opened at Gloucester on 7 November 1885 with Mr Justice Field presiding. Mr Charles Darling (who was later to become a judge) and the Hon. A. Lyttleton appeared for the Crown and, while the judge requested Mr Ram to appear in defence of John Hill, John Williams was defended by Mr Griffiths and Mr Cranston. Throughout the legal proceedings against him, John Williams had received both spiritual and financial assistance from Father Benedict Mackey, the Roman Catholic priest of Weobley, and it was he who had raised sufficient funds for Williams' defence. Father Mackey had attended the inquest and all the magistrates' hearings in support of Williams and was also present at his trial.

The sheer brutality of the murder of Ann Dickson, coupled with the fact that her death had left her five-year-old daughter motherless, had outraged the citizens of Weobley to the extent that they were most keen to see the two defendants convicted. Long before the trial was due to commence, people tried to push their way into the court, which was already filled to capacity. One area of the court had been set aside exclusively for female spectators, the judge having ruled on the previous day that they should not be excluded on account of the obscene and disgusting nature of the evidence likely to be presented in court.

It was the contention of the prosecution that the jury should have no difficulty in finding a verdict of wilful murder against both defendants, since the facts of the case were very plain. Mr Darling insisted that, even if the original intention of the defendants had been to rape either Ann Dickson or Mary Ann Farrell or both women, the fact that Ann Dickson had died during the course of this felonious act made both men equally responsible for her wilful murder.

Taking Hill's case first, Mr Darling reminded the jury that Hill had admitted that he was with the two women when Mary Ann Farrell was first stuck down. Shortly before Ann Dickson's death, Hill had changed into his Sunday-best clothes, which were then clean. Immediately after the murder, Hill had fled to Newport and, when he was arrested, his clean clothes were covered in mud and blood and there was even blood on the inside of his trousers. Where had that blood come from, asked Darling? Most damning of all was the fact that, at some time during the murderous attack on her, Ann Dickson had evacuated her bowels and, on his arrest, it was noted that the front of John Hill's shirt was smeared with faeces.

Witnesses who had seen Hill at the Red Lion Inn with Mary Ann Farrell and Ann Dickson on the night of the murder had testified to the fact that Hill's face and hands bore no scratches. On his arrest, both his face and hands were badly scratched and human skin had been found beneath the fingernails of the dead woman. Finally, Hill had written to his brother asking for money as he needed to get away from England as soon as he could.

Darling then asked the jury to consider the evidence against John Williams. He too had mud and blood on the clothes he was wearing on the night of the murder. If he had been the person who had hit and then tried to rape Mary Ann Farrell, it was to be expected that there would have been less mud on his clothes, since the attack on Mary Ann took place on a patch of grass. Admittedly, Mary Ann Farrell had bled when she was attacked but not enough to produce the amount of blood found on Williams' clothing.

Most importantly, the knobbed stick belonging to Williams had been found at the scene of the murder.

Darling told the jury that he didn't know whether Williams had attacked Ann Dickson while Mary Ann Farrell was lying stunned from the blow he had just dealt her or whether, having run away from the shepherd's cottage, he had returned to assist John Hill in his attack on Ann Dickson. Yet, Darling insisted, the order of events didn't matter because either way, Williams was guilty of the murder along with Hill.

The two defence counsels then spoke on behalf of their clients. Mr Ram had little to say in Hill's defence, pointing out only that the broken stick found at the scene of the crime indisputably belonged to John Williams. Thus, in order to have used it to kill Ann Dickson, Hill would either have had to take the stick from Williams or have it given to him by Williams. According to the *Hereford Times*, Ram then sat down again '...with the air of a brave man who had done his best.'

Mr Griffiths was much more eloquent in his defence of John Williams. He first of all stressed to the jury that his client was not on trial for the attack on Mary Ann Farrell but for the murder of Ann Dickson and there was absolutely no evidence to implicate him in Ann's death. When he was arrested on the morning after the murder, Williams had not denied that he was with Mary Ann Farrell the night before. However, he had denied striking Ann Dickson, saying that he knew who had struck the blow that killed her. Who else could Williams have seen but John Hill?

The mud on Williams' trousers could easily have come from a fall while struggling with Mary Ann Farrell, even if the original attack on her was perpetrated on grass. As for the blood, he had walked Mary Ann to the shepherd's cottage half supporting her, his arm around her waist. Where was his stick then?

The evidence at the scene of the crime, the fact that Ann Dickson had been dragged rather than carried and the imprints around the sites of the struggles suggested that one man – and only one man – had been involved. Furthermore, no excrement had been found on John Williams and neither did he have any scratches on his hands and face.

At this, the judge asked for surgeon Mr Walker to be recalled and Walker testified that there had in fact been six small scratches on Williams' right hand, although he was not prepared to swear that they had been caused by human fingernails.

Mary Ann Farrell (from a sketch in court). (Courtesy of the Hereford Times*)*

John Hill (from a sketch in court). (Courtesy of the Hereford Times*)*

John Williams (from a sketch in court). (Courtesy of the Hereford Times*)*

Griffiths concluded his defence of Williams by reminding the jury that, unlike Hill, Williams had made no effort to flee the area in the aftermath of the murder and had in fact been apprehended while sleeping peacefully in his own bed.

After the judge had summed up the evidence, the jury retired for only three minutes before returning a 'Guilty' verdict on both men. Saying that he agreed with the jury's conclusions, Field immediately picked up the square of black silk that had been lying prominently on his bench throughout the trial and sentenced both men to death.

Both men accepted the sentence without flinching and were sent back to Hereford Gaol. Meanwhile rumours abounded around the area that, on one of his voyages abroad, Hill had murdered a man in India and had only escaped justice by disguising himself with tar and fleeing back to his ship. It was also rumoured that Mary Ann Farrell had been troubled by recurring dreams in which Ann Dickson appeared to her, insisting that Hill alone was her murderer.

Williams continued to maintain his innocence until the very end, although Hill made a confession of sorts to the vicar of Weobley, placing the blame for the murder of Ann Dickson squarely on Williams' shoulders. Hill told the vicar that, having witnessed the attack on Mary Ann Farrell, Ann Dickson screamed and tried to run for the police. Hill detained her and had then tried to rape her, which she resisted violently. When Williams returned from the shepherd's cottage, he realised that Ann Dickson had Hill's thumb in her mouth and was biting down hard on it. He had hit her hard with his stick and, when she released his thumb, Hill insisted that he had picked up his hat from the ground and run away, leaving Williams and Dickson together. According to Hill, he had never struck Ann Dickson once, either with a stick or his fists.

Hill wrote numerous letters to his family during his incarceration in which he denied being guilty of murder but admitted having assaulted Ann Dickson. He blamed drink for his predicament, urging his brothers to avoid it at all costs.

Father Mackey made strenuous efforts to secure a reprieve for John Williams, pointing out in a letter to the Secretary of State what he saw as 'various omissions and discrepancies' in the trial and also writing to Mr Justice Field. Mackey was granted an interview at the Home Office but subsequently received a letter from the assistant under-secretary telling him that, although the Secretary of State had most carefully weighed up the papers and statements that Mackey had submitted to him, he saw no reason to recommend to Her Majesty any interference with the normal course of the law.

Shortly before the scheduled date of the execution, the families of both men were allowed to visit them in prison to bid them a last goodbye. It was doubtless an emotional time for all but particularly for the elderly mother of John Williams, who begged warders to be allowed to kiss her son through the bars of his cell. Her request was granted and she told her son that she hoped his spirit would go to heaven and that she would not be long in joining him there.

The double execution of Hill and Williams was the first ever private execution to be held at Hereford Prison. The appointed executioner was James Berry and, contrary to normal execution protocol, Berry didn't peer secretly through a spy hole at the prisoners in order to calculate his drops. Instead, he walked into their cells and introduced himself to Hill and Williams as the man who would 'launch them into eternity'.

Berry was later to describe Hill as the worst of the two men – an evil fellow with a hang-dog look and a bulging brow. Hill questioned Berry about the execution, cracking jokes and wondering aloud what drop Berry planned to give him. Berry was astounded by Hill's attitude and was later to say disapprovingly that he believed Hill should have been more concerned with his personal preparations to meet his Maker than with Berry's preparations to bring about that meeting. However, at one point, Hill's brave façade slipped and he asked Berry worriedly, 'Will it hurt?'

In the event, when the time for the execution arrived on 23 November 1885, Hill walked briskly towards the gallows unassisted, while Williams quaked with fear, needing the support of two warders. As the noose was placed around his neck, he continually beseeched, 'Jesus, have mercy on me.'

Notable for his absence at the execution was Williams' spiritual advisor and friend, Father Mackey. Mackey remained convinced of Williams' innocence and couldn't bear to watch what he believed to be a gross miscarriage of justice.

Note: The name of Mr Rogers' farm is recorded as both Homme and Holme Farm. (The local newspapers tend to use Homme Farm, while the nationals use Holme.) Ann Dickson is also sometimes named Sarah Ann Dickson and, in some accounts, her surname is alternatively spelled Dixon.

15

'I WONDER IF THE OLD MAN WILL GET OVER IT'

Tupsley, 1887

Note: The surviving accounts of this case in the local newspapers are of rather poor quality and some of the names are now almost illegible. This applies particularly to the accounts of the trial and thus, on occasions, I have been forced to make my 'best guesses' at the spelling of the names of some of the court personnel and key witnesses.

In October 1887, Miss Ada Ballard was visiting her uncle, Phillip, at his home at The Knoll, Tupsley. Mr Ballard, who was eighty-seven years old, was a talented artist, who had been employed first as a china painter, then as an enameller. However, years of staring into a hot fire while the enamel was burned took its toll on Ballard's eyesight and he was eventually forced to retire. Ballard then joined his younger brother, Stephen, who was the engineer and manager of the Herefordshire and Gloucester Canal, engaged in the construction of the Ledbury-Hereford segment of the waterway. When Stephen Ballard switched his focus to building railways, a job which involved lengthy absences from home, his brother took on his role and, when Stephen retired in 1840, Phillip was officially elected to fill his vacancy in the company, a position he still held.

Although Phillip Ballard no longer actually worked, a clever business deal meant that he still drew an annual salary from the business. Some years earlier, the ownership of the canal had been transferred to the Great Western Railway Company, who had filled in the section running from Gloucester to Ledbury and built a railway line. Instead of making an outright sale to the railway, Ballard had negotiated a share deal for his company, which received an annual payment, with interest at seven and a half per cent on their shares. Thus, although the canal company had ceased to be in all but name, Phillip Ballard was still officially the company clerk and received a handsome salary.

Thus Ballard was believed to be a wealthy man and was rumoured to keep large sums of money in the house. Known as a kindly man and well respected by all who knew him, in his later years, he largely shunned contact with the public and devoted himself almost entirely to his painting – even so, he was a sprightly old man, in very good health for his age, and still regularly walked into Hereford and back two or three times a week.

The tales of the substantial fortune allegedly kept at The Knoll undoubtedly triggered the events of 19/20 October 1887. By eleven o'clock that evening, the whole household had retired to bed. Ada slept in a room adjoining that of Mr Ballard, while Ballard's housekeeper, Margaret Weaver, slept in a bedroom opposite. There was one other servant in the house, a maid, Emily Emms, and one more houseguest – Emily's sister, Bessie, who was visiting at the time and sharing Margaret Weaver's bedroom.

In the early hours of the morning of 20 October, Margaret was disturbed from her sleep by the sound of somebody groaning. When she went to investigate, she spotted a very faint light downstairs, although as soon as she called out, the light immediately disappeared. Margaret followed the groaning noises to Phillip Ballard's bedroom, where she found the old man lying in his bed, covered in blood.

Margaret roused the rest of the household and sent Emily to fetch a near neighbour, the Revd Thomas Canning, while Ada Ballard hurried to wet a cloth, which she applied to her uncle's bleeding head. On leaving the house to fetch Canning, Emily noticed that both the back door and the scullery window were open, even though she had closed both before retiring to bed.

After quickly assessing the situation, Canning sent his coachman to fetch a doctor and returned to his own home to gather up lint and bandages to bind Mr Ballard's wounds.

When surgeon Mr Turner M.R.C.S. of Hereford arrived at about half-past two, he found that the blood drenching Mr Ballard originated from two severe wounds, one on each side of his forehead, the largest of which was three and a half inches long. Ballard was lying semi-conscious on his back in bed, moaning and throwing his arms about, occasionally muttering a few intelligible words, such as 'take it off'. In spite of his critical injuries, the old man clung to life for several days and, after his death, it was found that his skull was fractured beneath both of his wounds and his temporal artery severed. Mr Turner had no hesitation in pronouncing the wounds on Mr Ballard's head as being the cause of his death.

Nobody in the Ballard household had heard any sounds of a disturbance on the night of 19/20 October and the dog, which was sleeping in the dining room, had not barked. Nevertheless, it was obvious that the house had been burgled, as the cupboards and drawers had been turned out and their contents scattered about the house. A steel jemmy, or 'screw pinch', lay on a dressing table in Mr Ballard's bedroom, while a bloodstained hatchet was found in a downstairs room, next to where Mr Ballard's safe was located. Several items had been stolen, including three rings belonging to Margaret Weaver, which she had left in a downstairs room. Also missing were a concertina, a black frock coat, a white-faced gold watch with chain and seal, a silver bracelet, some keys and a white silk handkerchief. A distinctive pair of shoes that had been specially made in different sizes for Mr Ballard, to accommodate a large bunion on one of his feet, was also stolen.

Over the next few weeks, several of Mr Ballard's belongings were found in the area surrounding the house. The concertina was found in a field near Tupsley and handed to the police, as were a field glass and some opera glasses. A bunch of keys were found on 14 November in a meadow near Ballard's house and the coat was found the next day, partly submerged in a brook near Cradley. Two children each separately found one of a pair of clogs, which were handed to the police. There was coal dust on the clogs and one of them bore what looked like a bloodstain.

The police quickly arrested a Birmingham man named Moseley, the boyfriend of Emily Emms. After being remanded in custody for a few days, Moseley was eventually released without charge. Naturally, reports of the burglary-turned-murder appeared in the newspapers of the time, with a list of the stolen items and, just over a week after the incident, Chief Constable Frank Richardson of the Hereford Constabulary received a letter that was dated 'Oct 27, 1887'. The letter read:

> Sir – I take the liberty of writing these few lines to you. I see the accounts of that affair that happened at your place in to Days paper and I should like to know whether you have any other clue to that than there is in to days paper has I saw a man with precisely the same things in his possession for sale and I am certain that I can identify him if you think it would be of any service. you will consider this over and I tell you more if you think it is of any good. pleas send A telegram to the telegraph office Manchester by eleven Oclock on tomorrow morning to be left until called for and if not I shall think no more about it. Yours &c J. Beebe. [*sic*]

Richardson sent the telegram, as requested, but also telegraphed the Manchester police, asking them to intercept the writer of the letter. When Joseph Beebe arrived at the post office to collect the response, the police were there waiting for him. Beebe willingly gave a statement, no doubt encouraged by the £100 reward offered by Ballard's family for information leading to the apprehension of his killer(s). However, Beebe was unwilling to give his address to the Manchester police, with good reason – he was wanted by the Birmingham police on a charge of robbery. Eventually, the lure of the reward money was too great for Beebe to resist and he returned to Birmingham, where he served a short prison sentence. On his release, he was deemed eligible for the reward.

Beebe told the police in Manchester that, on 20 October, he had been living in a house in Park Street, Birmingham. At about nine o'clock that night, a man had come to the house. He was obviously known to one of the occupants, who asked him where he had been lately, to which the man replied that he had been serving time in gaol and had just been released that morning. The man then produced a number of items including a white-faced gold watch with a chain and seal, a white silk handkerchief with a flower pattern and a thick gold ring.

Beebe told the man that he could get into trouble but the man assured him that he had done his time and that 'they' couldn't hurt him now. Saying that he had hidden the items before he went into gaol, the man said that he had more things in his pockets and wished he could sell them all. He offered to sell Beebe the handkerchief for 1s, an offer which Beebe declined. Having had no luck selling his booty, the man left the lodging house at between midnight and 1 a.m. and Beebe had never seen him again.

Mr Green, who owned the lodging house in Park Street, confirmed Beebe's account and both men believed that they could identify the man if they saw him again. Based on their recollections, the police issued a description of the wanted man who was in his mid to late twenties, 5ft 3 or 4ins tall, clean shaven with a fresh complexion and dark brown hair. At the time of his visit to Birmingham, he was wearing a black coat and vest, corduroy trousers and a black pot hat.

As the investigations into Mr Ballard's murder continued, more witnesses came forward. A man matching the description given by Beebe had bought the jemmy on 19 October at an ironmonger's in Ledbury, owned by John Davies. Davies routinely marked every item he sold and was thus able to say with absolute certainty that the jemmy found in Ballard's bedroom was the one he had sold in his shop.

The same man had also bought two third-class tickets from Ledbury station for a train travelling to Withington, which was less than four miles from Ballard's house. In the late afternoon, he and a companion called at the New Inn at Lugwardine, less than two miles from Tupsley, purchasing a quart of cider and asking the landlord, Hilo Williams, for some food, which he was unable to supply. The two men later bought two pennies' worth of biscuits at Mrs Buswell's shop in Lugwardine and were next seen at 6.30 p.m. leaning on a gate close to The Knoll by postman George Parry. Finally, shortly before midnight, they were seen within 500 yards of The Knoll by labourer James Soley.

Some of the witnesses were able to name the man as James Jones. Three or four years earlier, Jones had called on Phillip Ballard to collect an outstanding bill on behalf of his uncle, a blacksmith, and was thus familiar with both the house and Mr Ballard – and, no doubt, the rumours of the old gentleman's fortune. Jones had recently been incarcerated in Warwick Gaol and had only been freed on 18 October, along with another man, Alfred Scandrett.

On 4 November, Detective Sergeant Donovan of the Hereford police went to the home of James Jones' father, where he confronted Jones.

'Where's your mate?' Donovan asked him as he placed him under arrest.

'Haven't you arrested him?' asked Jones.

Jones was then charged with 'burglariously entering the home of Mr Ballard' on the morning of 20 October and stealing various items, also with murdering Mr Ballard. 'All I have to say is that I am not guilty of the crime,' responded Jones.

However, later that afternoon, while in custody, Jones apparently changed his mind and asked PC Bromage if he might have a pen, paper and a dictionary. When Bromage asked him why he wanted them, Jones told him, 'I am not going to stand all the blame.' Once he was given the pen and paper, James Jones wrote down and signed a full account of the events of the night of 19/20 October, in which he largely blamed his companion for the murder of Mr Ballard.

According to Jones, he and Scandrett had become acquainted in HMP Warwick and, on their release on 18 October, had decided together to burgle Mr Ballard's home. The two men had broken into the house by opening a window and Scandrett had picked up the hatchet, intending to use it to force open the internal doors.

Jones had seen Scandrett pocket several items, including the silk handkerchief, rings, bracelet and the pair of shoes. Scandrett had then headed upstairs, the hatchet still in his hand, telling Jones that he was gong to see if there was anything of value up there. Jones insisted that he had waited downstairs in the hall and had heard groans coming from an upstairs room. Scandrett had come back downstairs carrying a coat and a pair of new-looking boots, along with a bunch of keys. The men tried to open the safe with the keys, before leaving the house when they heard Margaret Weaver moving about upstairs.

Later that morning, Scandrett showed Jones a watch and chain he had stolen from upstairs and mused, 'I wonder if the old man will get over it.' When Jones asked him what he meant by that, Scandrett admitted to hitting Ballard twice on the head with the 'hacker'.

Jones wrote that Scandrett had discarded the clogs he had been wearing and replaced them with the boots he had stolen from Ballard's home. Shortly afterwards, the two men separated, each making his own way back to Birmingham, Scandrett taking the entire haul from the burglary. Jones swore that he was guilty of assisting Scandrett in breaking into the house but not of anything else.

Alfred Scandrett's portrait was posted in police stations in the area and a description of him issued, which stated that he was twenty-three years old, 5ft 3½ ins tall and 'of wild aspect'. Particular attention was drawn to his distinctive tattoos and to a deformity of his shoulders that left one higher than the other.

Scandrett was actually in Worcester and had made no attempt whatsoever at concealing himself while there. He attended a race meeting at Worcester racecourse and, after the race meeting, was seen and heard loudly singing Salvation Army hymns in the streets. In spite of his conspicuousness, the Worcester police did not succeed in finding him until they received information from a Mr Clement Dale, who had seen the wanted poster in the police station and recognised Scandrett as someone he had once known from Birmingham.

Dale's wife actually met Scandrett in Worcester and asked him if he knew that his portrait was being displayed in the police station in connection with Mr Ballard's murder. 'It is our kid,' Scandrett reassured her, referring to his brother and adding, 'I have been up and cleared myself this afternoon.'

Dale's information led the police to a lodging house in Worcester, where Scandrett gave them a false name, saying that he was Joseph Spriggs from Manchester. However, he was soon identified by his tattoos and his crooked shoulder.

Arrested and taken to Hereford, Scandrett made a statement in which he accused James Jones of the murder of Phillip Ballard. Scandrett's version of events was that both men had watched until they saw Mr Ballard walking round the house checking the doors in preparation for retiring for the night. Ballard had briefly stepped outside, something he was known to do on most evenings. Jones had been keen to 'knock the old man on the head' while he was outside but Scandrett said that he had pointed out that the old man was carrying a lamp and that it was likely to start a fire.

When all the lights in the house had been extinguished, Jones and Scandrett broke into the house, talking to the dog to ensure that it didn't bark. Then, said Scandrett, Jones led the way upstairs and into Mr Ballard's bedroom. When Ballard sat up and asked, 'What do you want?' Jones had struck him over the head with the hatchet. He had then suggested that they should also 'settle' the servants but Scandrett told him they had done enough. Having tried to open the safe, the men left the house and walked across the fields before separating.

While Jones had stated that Scandrett had taken all the stolen items for himself, Scandrett insisted that Jones had been intent on taking everything until he had admonished him, 'Don't be grabbish. You want it all,' and snatched some of the items out of his hands. They arranged to meet again at Bromsgrove but Scandrett stated that he had been unable to find Jones there so had walked to Birmingham alone, from where he had travelled to Worcester.

Scandrett seemed to view his capture with some relief, telling the police that he hadn't eaten for three days and was almost starved. Rather than being concerned or contrite, he treated his arrest with some levity, taking particular delight in the fact that he had picked the pocket of a police superintendent from Birmingham and taken his watch and chain. Interestingly, in the light of his strenuous denials of murdering Mr Ballard, he told the police that he had intended to give himself up, saying, 'I would not let an innocent fellow suffer for what I have done.' After appearing before magistrates in Worcester, he was taken by train to Hereford, where a large crowd booed him on his arrival at the railway station.

Both men were committed to stand trial at Hereford Assizes for the wilful murder of Phillip Ballard. The trial – which was to last three days – opened on 1 March 1888 before the Lord Chief Justice, Lord Coleridge. Mr Gresham Wells and Mr W.A. Wigram prosecuted the case, while the judge assigned defence counsels for both of the accused, Mr Moreton Browne acting for James Jones and Mr A. Chichele Plowden for Scandrett.

As soon as the proceedings opened, Browne requested that the two men should be tried separately. There was no objection, either from the prosecution or the prisoners, so Scandrett was taken from the court and James Jones was placed in the dock, where he immediately began to cry.

As far as the prosecution team were concerned, the cases against both Jones and Scandrett were quite straightforward and they insisted that, whichever one of them had struck the two blows that killed Phillip Ballard, both were equally responsible for the murder in the eyes of the law. The prosecution then proceeded to call numerous witnesses, all of whom testified to having seen the defendants in the area of The Knoll or to having been offered the items stolen from Mr Ballard's house.

When it was time for the defence counsels to speak, both focused on the statements their respective clients had made to the police on their arrests.

Mr Browne told the jury that he hoped that the fact that Jones had just been released from prison wouldn't prejudice their judgement on the case before them. It was not for him to prove that Jones did not commit the murder but for the prosecution to prove that he did and the evidence against his client, James Jones, was entirely circumstantial. Jones did not deny having been in the house that night with the intent to burgle, but continued to insist that he had been downstairs when Scandrett struck the fatal blows and had never set foot in Mr Ballard's bedroom.

The doctor had testified in court that he had found evidence of only two blows on Ballard's head and that both of those had been made with the hatchet. Jones had admitted to buying the jemmy but no blows had been struck with that weapon.

The clogs found in the fields by the two children after the murder were Scandrett's. They bore traces of coal dust and also what looked like a bloodstain. The hatchet, which belonged to Mr Ballard, was kept in the coal shed outside the house, suggesting that it had been Scandrett who was holding the hatchet and so dealt the fatal blows. Furthermore, none of the stolen items from the bedroom were ever found in Jones' possession.

Browne then went on to argue the legalities of both men being equally responsible for the murder in the eyes of the law when it had been clearly shown that only one of them actually struck the victim. 'It doesn't matter which struck the blow,' insisted the judge.

Browne was not convinced. He pointed out that the only thing the men had taken with them was the jemmy and that was clearly intended to be used as a tool to facilitate the burglary rather than as a weapon. If Scandrett had picked up a hatchet, then could his client be held responsible for what the other man decided to do with it? Asking the jury to give his client the benefit of any doubts they might have, the defence for James Jones rested.

When it came to Scandrett's turn in the dock, Mr Plowden told the jury that if the evidence against Jones was circumstantial, then the evidence against Scandrett was equally so.

It was Jones who knew the victim and it was he who had led his client into robbing the house. Scandrett was not a Hereford man but came from Birmingham and knew nothing about Mr Ballard and the legendary fortune that he kept at his house. Jones was familiar with the house and, in all probability, would have been more likely to know where the hatchet was kept than his accomplice. He was also the most likely to know which was Mr Ballard's bedroom. It was highly possible that Mr Ballard would have recognised him, giving him a motive to murder the old man rather than risk being identified as a burglar.

Scandrett's account of the events preceding the murder most closely tallied with the evidence given by members of Mr Ballard's household. Scandrett had stated that the two men had watched through the windows as Ada Ballard read to her uncle, which she had indeed done before retiring to bed on the night of the murder. Scandrett had also stated that Mr Ballard had briefly come outside before retiring, something he was known to be in the habit of doing. Finally, Plowden reminded the jury of a remark that Scandrett had made in his confession, when he related saying to Jones, 'If I had known as much as I do now, you would not have got me on this hop.' In other words, Scandrett would never have agreed to the burglary had he been aware that Jones was prepared to use violence against the victim.

On the final day of the trial, the judge took his seat at ten o'clock in the morning, the square of black silk clearly visible in his hand as he entered the courtroom. Before resuming the proceedings against Jones and Scandrett, the judge had another matter to address.

Calling the two court bailiffs, Mr Willis and Mr Lambourn, the judge informed them that he had heard that somebody who was not a member of the jury was with them on the previous evening. Was that true?

Both bailiffs admitted that it was. Neither of them knew the identity of the strange man who had walked into the Green Dragon Hotel where the jury had stayed overnight, supposedly being closely guarded by Willis and Lambourn. Lambourn ventured to say that he had thought at the time that the man was a hotel waiter but the judge was having none of his excuses. He fined both bailiffs £20 each and told them that, if they couldn't do their duty any better, he trusted that those who had appointed them would engage someone else who could. Eventually, the man was identified as William Smith, the butler to the Sheriff, who was also staying at the hotel. Smith was brought before the judge and, although he denied saying anything to the jury other than presenting them with a memorial of the case, he was promptly fined £10 for contempt of court. (It was variously reported in the local newspapers that the three were actually fined £50 each and also that the judge later relented and contented himself with a severe rebuke rather than a monetary penalty.)

The judge then summarised the evidence for the jury, paying particular attention to the legal issue of the equal responsibility of both men for the murder. The two prisoners had been heard talking about the case together in Hereford Gaol, although they had been advised several times not to do so, since they were not under caution.

The Green Dragon Hotel, Hereford, 1940s. (Author's collection)

The fact that the men had been discussing the case between them suggested that this was a joint venture and the law was abundantly clear on that matter. If two persons went to commit a felony and, in the course of that felony, one man took the life of another man, both men were guilty of murder, regardless of whether or not the second man had actually touched the victim. He might have been 100 yards away at the time of the murder but it was all part of the felony that the two had agreed to commit. The law stated, quoted the judge, 'If you go together to break the law and, in the breaking of that law, one of you takes a life, the man who goes along is as clearly guilty as the man who took the life.'

The jury needed less than five minutes to consider their verdicts on each of the two trials and found both defendants guilty of the wilful murder of Mr Phillip Ballard. Both men became extremely emotional as the judge pronounced the death sentence and Scandrett glared at Jones with an expression of pure hatred on his face. As the judge spoke, Scandrett began to rock backwards and forwards, sobbing piteously. His face slowly contorted and he fell into the warder's arms in a fit. Then suddenly, without any warning, Scandrett sprang towards Jones and it took three warders to wrestle him to the floor and prevent him from strangling Jones.

In the end, the job of despatching Jones was left to executioner James Berry, who executed both men in a double hanging at Hereford Gaol on 20 March 1888.

Twenty-five-year-old Scandrett was a native of Birmingham and a career criminal, with numerous charges of theft and burglary to his name. As a child, he had spent five years in a reformatory for stealing newspapers from New Street Station, since when he had served several prison sentences. Jones was four years younger and came from a very respectable family. Like Scandrett, he too had numerous previous convictions for arson, theft and burglary. Both men made a full confession to the prison chaplain, Revd G.L. Spencer, before their execution.

Fearing a repeat of the fight between the two men that had occurred during their trial, the two condemned men were assigned extra warders to escort them to the gallows. However, according to the contemporary newspaper reports, both walked to the gallows with a firm step, each completely ignoring the other and '...judging by their demeanour, no-one would have supposed that they had ever met before.'

Note: There is some discrepancy surrounding the servant, Emily, and her sister Bessie, who are variously named as Emms, Emma and Emme.

16

'HE IS AS MUCH AT LEAST OF A FOOL AS A KNAVE'

Little Hereford, 1891

Walter Frederick Steers was born in March 1889 and, for the first nine months of his life, he lived with his parents in London. When his mother fell ill and was consequently unable to look after him, Walter passed into the care of a Mrs Smith from Walsall, who later moved to Kidderminster, taking the child with her. Mrs Smith had custody of Walter for several months before she suffered a stroke, after which the little boy was sent to live with a Mrs Dixon. The child lived with Mrs Dixon for only a short while before being returned to Mrs Smith. Yet Mrs Smith was still far from well and for the next few months of his life, Walter was passed around like a parcel from foster home to foster home. It seemed that nobody wanted the poor little boy – until Elizabeth Caldwell came into his life.

Elizabeth was the daughter of a farm labourer from Thornbury, near Bromyard. After the death of her mother when Elizabeth was only a baby, her father struggled to care for his children properly while, at the same time, earning sufficient money to feed and clothe them and keep a roof over their heads. Elizabeth and her elder brother ran wild and she soon developed a reputation for promiscuity and petty crime.

Preferring to sleep under haystacks and in farm buildings to living in her father's tied cottage, Elizabeth soon found herself brought before magistrates on a charge of vagrancy. The magistrates sent her to live at the workhouse but she quickly discharged herself and took to a life of tramping around the country, picking up casual work when and where she could find it.

While working on a farm pulling swedes, Elizabeth met fellow labourer Charles Sanders. Sanders was the son of a very respectable family. His father worked in a porcelain factory in Worcester for many years and owned a small general shop. Yet in spite of his upbringing, by the time he met Elizabeth, thirty-one-year-old Charles already had an extensive criminal record.

It began in 1879, with a charge of stealing pears. Over the next few years, Sanders served several short prison sentences, mostly for stealing or obtaining money by false pretences. In 1883, having just been released from prison after serving a nine-month sentence, he was arrested for stealing 2s and, as a habitual offender, was awarded a relatively harsh sentence of five years' imprisonment. Released on a ticket of leave after three years, his freedom was conditional on him regularly reporting to the police and, when he failed to do so, he was returned to prison to finish his sentence. Finally freed in January 1889, he too adopted a vagabond's life, roaming around the countryside taking various casual jobs including working the swing boats in a travelling fair and hop picking.

Towards the end of 1890, his wanderings took him to Bromyard, where he met Elizabeth Caldwell. Sanders soon persuaded Elizabeth to 'forsake her home, family and friends and throw in her lot with his.' Together the couple headed for Kidderminster, arriving there in mid-April of 1891. Elizabeth soon spotted Walter Steers sitting in a chair in a house.

Walter was a beautiful little boy with fair hair and big blue eyes and Elizabeth immediately recognised his potential. 'That will get us many a living and clothes,' she told Sanders.

Sanders was not quite so keen to saddle himself with the burden of a child but he could see the financial sense in Elizabeth's words. Eventually her pleading won the day and he allowed her to walk into the house and pick up the little boy, walking out with him unchallenged.

For the next two weeks, little Walter was carted around the countryside by Caldwell and Sanders, used as a 'prop' to tug at the heartstrings of those members of the public from whom the couple made their living by begging. The child led a miserable existence at the hands of a couple whose only interest in child rearing came from the recognition that there was money to be made from the toddler's presence.

Within days, Walter was emaciated and covered in sores and bruises, many resulting from the smacks that his new foster parents doled out at all too regular intervals. Sanders quickly tired of what he saw as the constant demands of childcare and began to amuse himself by perpetrating some of the cruellest abuse imaginable on the helpless little boy. On one occasion, when the child seemed hungry, Sanders offered him the hot bowl of his tobacco pipe to suckle and on another occasion, Sanders thrust a stick down little Walter's throat. Urged by several people to treat the child's scabs and sores, Sanders obtained some white grease which he rubbed all over Walter's face. He then held the little boy on his knee, positioning Walter's face directly over the fire in order to melt the grease into his skin.

Astonishingly, although there were numerous witnesses to Sanders' ill-treatment of the child, not one person thought to intervene on the boy's behalf or even remonstrate with the couple on their abusive behaviour.

The one exception was Mrs Higgins, the wife of a farm labourer from Ashford Carbonel. When Walter was brought to the village by Sanders and Caldwell, Mrs Higgins was appalled at his condition. As well as being covered in sores, Walter was by now filthy, stinking and starving hungry. Mrs Higgins offered to care for the child and was permitted by Sanders to wash him and dress him in clean clothes outgrown by her own children, having first treated his terrible skin lesions with healing salve. Once he was clean, Mrs Higgins not only fed him but also provided his foster parents with food.

On 1 May 1891, Sanders did some casual labour on a farm in Little Hereford but was forced to stop work when it began to rain heavily. Taking the sixpence he had been paid for his morning's toil, he and Elizabeth decided that it was high time they had some fun and so, taking Walter with them, they walked to the May Fair at nearby Ludlow.

The pseudo family returned to Little Hereford late that night and took possession of an empty cottage. However, by that time, little Walter was doubtless tired and hungry and began to grizzle and cry for his 'Mama'. The child's crying soon began to grate on Charles Sanders, preventing him from sleeping and, having tried several times to quieten Walter by smacking him, Sanders eventually seized the little boy by the legs in a fit of rage, shook him violently and then threw him across the room onto the floor.

Walter's crying ceased immediately. Elizabeth Caldwell, who had watched the whole episode, promptly fainted and, when she came round, Walter was ominously silent. Elizabeth urged Sanders to call a surgeon for the child but Sanders flatly refused, threatening to treat Elizabeth in the same way if she defied him. Pausing only to cover Walter's body with straw in an attempt to conceal it, Sanders and Elizabeth picked up their belongings and fled to Worcester.

Walter's body lay undiscovered until 23 August. The cottage was untenanted and on that day an itinerant farm labourer went to check on some apparently unwanted potatoes that were growing in the garden. Finding the cottage door unsecured, he couldn't resist looking around inside, where he soon found what he believed was the badly decomposed body of a child. He reported his discovery to his employer, Mr Edwin Froggatt, and, first thing the following morning, Froggatt accompanied the labourer back to the cottage to investigate. Having satisfied himself that there was indeed a body there, Froggatt notified the police.

Walter's body was so badly decomposed that it was initially thought that he was a little girl and it was only at a post-mortem examination that his true gender was determined. Given the appalling decomposition of the child's remains, the surgeons who conducted the post-mortem examination could find nothing whatsoever to suggest that the child had not died a natural death. Although the coroner's jury at the subsequent inquest recorded a verdict of 'death due to bowel disorder arising from irregular feeding and neglect', the police strongly suspected foul play, particularly since no children had been reported missing from the area in recent months. The Chief Constable of Leominster was especially keen to find an explanation for the child's death and set one of his officers, Superintendent Strangward, the task of solving the mystery.

In order to try and establish Walter's identity, his clothes were removed and washed. Walter was found wearing a red quilted petticoat, a mauve cape, a violet frock, a white flannel petticoat, an embroidered linen chemise, nearly new black wool socks, leather buttoned boots and a flannelette cap.

The clothing was obviously of very good quality and was soon recognised by Mrs Higgins as the garments she had given to the tramping family some months earlier. She was able to give Strangward an excellent description of the couple she believed to have been the little boy's parents and police forces throughout the Midlands were alerted to be on the lookout for anybody who might fit the bill.

Meanwhile, Elizabeth and Sanders had moved to Worcester and their relationship had ended. Tired of suffering constant physical abuse at his hands, Elizabeth finally left Sanders and was admitted to Worcester Infirmary for treatment for the injuries he had caused her. Once discharged, she made her way back to her home village of Thornbury, where she was arrested and charged with the wilful murder of Walter Steers.

Without Elizabeth as a steadying influence, Sanders had quickly reverted to his previous criminal lifestyle, this time committing a far more serious offence than his usual thefts and deceptions. When Mary Ann Weaver, whose parents kept the Eagle Inn in Pheasant Street, Worcester, went for a Sunday afternoon walk with some other children, Sanders lured the seven-year-old girl away from her friends and into some empty stables. Producing a knife, he threatened to kill her unless she submitted to his demands and then proceeded to indecently assault her, carrying out what the newspapers of the day described as 'a brutal outrage'.

The courageous little girl was later able to identify her attacker and Sanders was arrested and charged, eventually being committed by magistrates for trial at the Worcester Assizes. (There is some evidence that, at the same time, he was also charged with assault on Elizabeth Caldwell.) It was at this stage that the Worcester police received a communication from Strangward about the suspects wanted in connection with the death of Walter Steers and realised that they probably had the man in their custody. On the same day that Elizabeth Caldwell was arrested in Thornbury, Strangward received a telegram from his colleagues, telling him that his fugitive was about to be tried for a criminal assault on Mary Ann Weaver.

The Herefordshire case took priority, particularly as Elizabeth Caldwell had now made a statement accusing Sanders of the murder of Walter Steers. It was decided to charge Charles Sanders with murder and to drop all charges against Elizabeth Caldwell in order to allow her to act as a witness against him since, without her testimony, the police actually had very little evidence to connect Sanders with Walter's death. Sanders made his own statement to the police in which he admitted being irritated by Walter's constant crying and to shaking the child in a passion. While shaking the child, he had accidentally knocked the boy's head on a brick. However, this statement was in contrast to remarks he had made before his arrest, having then admitted to several people that he had deliberately dashed the child's head against the floor of the cottage to try and shut him up.

After a hearing at Leominster Petty Sessions, Sanders was committed for trial at the next Herefordshire Assizes. The trial opened before Mr Justice Day on 3 December 1891, with Mr Marshal Todd and Mr R.E.C. Kettle prosecuting and Mr Richard Harington acting for Charles Sanders, who pleaded 'Not Guilty' to the charge of wilful murder against him.

It must be remembered that, at the inquest into the death of Walter Steers, the coroner's jury had returned a verdict of 'death due to bowel disorder arising from irregular feeding and neglect' rather than one of wilful murder. It was also the case that the doctors who performed the post-mortem on the child had found no indication whatsoever that the child's death was due to anything but natural causes.

Thus, as the trial progressed, Sanders must have held out hopes of an acquittal, especially when Elizabeth Caldwell, the prosecution's chief witness, gave her testimony. Having related her account of the events of the early hours of the morning of 2 May, Elizabeth was forced to admit that it had been so dark in the cottage at the time that she had not actually seen the child's head hit anything.

Old magistrates' court, Leominster. (© N. Sly)

Charles Sanders, from a portrait taken in gaol.
This picture was reproduced in the Hereford
Times *in December 1891. (Courtesy of the*
Hereford Times)

In anticipation of a defence of insanity, the prosecution team had obtained a full medical report on Charles Sanders. However, the question of Sanders' mental state at the time of the murder was never raised. Instead, Mr Harington made an impassioned speech in defence of his client. Dealing first with the allegations of cruelty to little Walter against Sanders, he dismissed these as 'absurd fables'. He found it impossible to believe that any witness would just stand by and watch a man thrust a stick into a child's throat or place the hot bowl of a pipe in its mouth without intervening to protect the child concerned. Pointing out that the medical evidence presented in court had satisfactorily proved that Walter's death was due to natural causes, Harington told the court that he was not disputing the fact that Sanders' actions had directly contributed to the boy's demise. However, Harington maintained that, at very worst, his client should only have been charged with manslaughter.

In his summary of the evidence for the jury, Mr Justice Day reminded them that although the defendant had admitted only to accidentally striking the child's head in his statement to the police, he had previously made statements to two women in which he specifically said that he had dashed Walter's head against the floor.

It was with this thought in their minds that the jury retired, returning after half an hour to pronounce Charles Sanders 'Guilty' of the wilful murder of Walter Frederick Steers.

Sanders was described in the newspapers of the time as a short man, with a deep, overhanging forehead, sunken eyes, a small nose, hollow cheeks and 'a cast of countenance of a criminal character.' Throughout the eight-hour trial, he sat quietly on a chair in the dock, leaning forward every now and again to whisper something to his defence counsel. It was only when the judge began to pronounce the death sentence that Sanders first appeared to realise what was happening, at which he burst into noisy tears, sobbing bitterly as he was removed from the court to the condemned cell at Hereford Gaol. He was so anguished that he was placed under constant watch in the run-up to his execution.

Such was the public horror and outrage at the brutal killing of an innocent child aged just two years and eight months, that there was no attempt to petition for clemency for Sanders. Indeed, Sanders seemed to have just one remaining ally in the world – the Honourable and Reverend Henry Douglas of St Paul's Church in Worcester.

Douglas wrote a letter of appeal in which he stated that he had known Charles Sanders for many years and felt that he was a man of weak intellect. 'He is as much at least of a fool as a knave,' wrote Douglas, adding,

> He was here at my house more than once in the month of July last and a more civil, docile creature on those days there could not be. His outward form was vastly against him. His whole expression suggested moral ubiquity, arising from immoral association, weakness of character and intellect, blunting his moral perceptions and making him not wholly responsible for his actions under circumstances of temptation or of momentary vexation.

On hearing of this letter, the *Hereford Times* asked somewhat incredulously, 'Has then the condemned man a dual personality such as the psychologists describe? Or is he a man in whom brute instincts have become predominant?' Whatever the answer to those questions, the letter from Revd Douglas was not acted upon and Charles Sanders went to the gallows.

The actual date of his execution at Hereford Gaol is variously recorded as being on 24, 29 and 30 December 1891. In the early morning, crowds began to assemble before the prison on Commercial Road, expecting the execution to take place at eight o'clock.

A few minutes before the hour, there was a loud thumping noise from within the prison and, believing the sound to be that of the trapdoors below the noose dropping, the crowd surged forward to witness the ritual hoisting of the black flag outside the prison. Yet, as the minutes past, no flag fluttered on the prison flagpole. The crowd began to get restless. Was there a problem inside the prison? Had the prisoner been reprieved?

Eventually, the prison doctor, Mr Henry Vevers, was seen emerging from the building and was almost instantly surrounded by people asking him what had happened. The doctor explained that executioner James Billington, who had been engaged to hang Sanders, should have reported to the prison on the previous afternoon but, as yet, had not arrived. In anticipation of the arrival of the first train from Worcester, the execution had now been postponed until half-past nine.

Although the train was a few minutes late, Billington was indeed a passenger and he was rushed to the prison by hansom cab, arriving there at about a quarter past nine. Once again, the crowd assembled in anticipation and once again a loud crash was heard from within the confines of the prison. Yet there was still no black flag hoisted and, after a couple of minutes the crashing sound was repeated. Only then was the black flag finally raised to mark Sanders' death.

Note: There are various discrepancies in contemporary newspaper accounts of the murder. The variation in the date of the execution has already been mentioned and, although different sources give different dates, most seem to agree that it occurred on a Wednesday morning, which would suggest that 30 December is the correct date. Elizabeth Caldwell's name is alternatively spelled Caldwall and most newspapers initially refer to the murderer as Charles Saunders, later correcting the name to Sanders.

17

'I AM AFRAID I'VE LOST HER'

Pokehouse Quarry, near Leominster, 1903

Saturday, 11 July 1903, was oppressively hot and sunny and as the day came to an end many people took advantage of the slightly cooler conditions and went out for an evening stroll in the Herefordshire countryside, just to get a breath of fresh air. At about a quarter past nine, a man in working clothes came walking along the footpath leading from Pokehouse limestone quarry towards Mortimers Cross Mill, near Leominster. The man was pushing a wheelbarrow and passers-by were shocked to see that the barrow contained the body of an elderly woman.

When the man was challenged by labourer John Davies, he initially denied that the woman – his wife – was dead. He explained that she had met with an unfortunate accident at his place of work and that he was taking her home. By now, quite a crowd had gathered around the man and his wheelbarrow and somebody suggested that the woman should be removed from her makeshift hearse to determine whether or not life was actually extinct. Accordingly, the woman's body was gently lifted from the barrow and laid on a patch of grass.

It was immediately obvious to everyone present that the woman was beyond any assistance. Scantily clad and drenched from head to toe in blood, there was a large, gaping wound in her head above one ear. Her right arm hung at an impossible angle and her left leg was so badly broken below her knee that the splintered bone had actually forced itself outwards through her flesh.

The man was detained and the police and a doctor were summoned. While waiting for their arrival, the man quietly lay down on the grass next to his wife's body, occasionally remarking that he wished he was her and saying that perhaps he had better go and drown himself. When PC Preece of Kingsland arrived at the scene he asked the man what had happened.

'I am afraid I've lost her,' the man replied dolefully, before suddenly leaping to his feet and making a desperate run towards the river Lugg. He was quickly tackled and brought to the ground before he could reach his goal.

Taken to Leominster police station, sixty-one-year-old William Haywood from Yarpole continued to insist that his wife's death had been a tragic accident. Haywood worked for Leominster Rural District Council as a quarryman and his wife, Jane, frequently assisted him in his work. He told the police that, while he was throwing stones out of the quarry, one had hit his 'old woman' on the head and he had been unable to stop the bleeding. However the post-mortem examination on the body of fifty-nine-year-old Jane Haywood told a very different story.

Dr Robert Williams found that in addition to the large wound on her head, Jane Haywood was covered in huge, black bruises all over her face and body. Her arms and hands were particularly badly affected, as if she had raised them to try to protect her head against an onslaught of blows. Her right arm was broken near to her elbow and her left leg was fractured in two places. She had also been the victim of what the newspapers of the time described as 'a ferocious and grotesque indignity of an indescribable kind.' Williams concluded that Jane had been either brutally beaten or kicked to death and, when the police visited Pokehouse Quarry where, according to her husband, Jane had met with her 'accident', the evidence found there seemed to support the doctor's findings. There were splashes of blood liberally scattered over the entire area, as well as a large pool of blood under a young oak tree. The police found several bloodstained sticks, as well as what was described in the contemporary newspapers as a 'bloodied hacker'.

The police began to piece together the movements of both William and Jane Haywood on the days immediately preceding her death and their findings emerged

Mortimers Cross Inn.
(© R. Sly)

at the inquest opened by coroner Mr C.E.A. Moore at the Mortimers Cross Inn. (The proceedings were later adjourned and resumed at a different location in nearby Kingsland.)

The couple had six children, three sons and three daughters, of whom only one, Elizabeth, was still living at home. Elizabeth told the police that, on the day before her mother's death, her father did not go to work but spent most of the afternoon drinking in the Bell Inn at Yarpole. Eventually Jane was forced to go to the pub to try and persuade her husband to come home for his supper.

William was furious at this intrusion and refused to accompany her home. Some time later, Jane went back to the pub and again her husband angrily sent her away, although he did leave the pub shortly afterwards. After eating his meal, having first told Jane in no uncertain terms exactly what he thought of her, he announced his intention of sleeping at the quarry in order to get an early start on his work before the expected hot weather of the following day. The next morning, Jane left the house just before eight o'clock to walk to the quarry with some breakfast for her husband – it was to be the last time that Elizabeth was to see her mother alive.

Meanwhile, having spent the previous night at the quarry, William visited the Mortimers Cross Inn at seven o'clock on the morning of 11 July. He drank a pint of beer and also bought another pint bottle of beer as well as a bottle of whisky, which he took away with him. (The two empty bottles were later found at the quarry.)

At one o'clock Haywood was back at the Mortimers Cross Inn where, according to witnesses, he seemed sober, if a little dazed. Complaining bitterly about the heat, he bought a pint of beer and casually mentioned to the other drinkers that his 'old

The Bell Inn,
Yarpole.
(© N. Sly)

woman' had met with an accident at the quarry. He explained that he had been throwing stones out of the quarry and one had hit his wife behind her ear, cutting her head open and that he was unable to stop the bleeding. It was suggested that it would be a good idea to fetch a doctor for the injured woman and William seemed to agree. He immediately left the pub and the other drinkers presumed that he had heeded their advice and was going to seek medical help for his wife. 'If she's dead when I get back, I'll bury her in the brook,' was his parting remark.

William was back at the quarry by two o'clock without having sought the services of a doctor. He was seen from a distance apparently fetching water from the river Lugg in a bucket then was next seen trundling his wheelbarrow homewards later that evening.

The coroner's jury recorded a verdict of wilful murder against William Haywood, who was committed to stand trial at the next Hereford Assizes. His trial was held before Mr Justice Bigham on 28 November 1903 with Mr Stanford Hutton and Mr Reginald Coventry prosecuting. At the request of the judge, Mr S.R.C. Bosanquet appeared in defence of Haywood, who pleaded 'Not Guilty' to the charge against him.

It emerged in court that Haywood had a history of violence towards his wife and children and that, some years earlier, he had served a term in prison having been convicted of a criminal assault on one of his daughters. Although only William Haywood knew exactly what had transpired in the quarry on 11 July, the prosecution surmised that he had turned on his wife in a drunken frenzy and ferociously battered her to death.

The counsel for the defence had very little option open to him other than trying to demonstrate that William Haywood was insane at the time he killed his wife. Bosanquet told the court that the peculiar ferocity and senselessness of the crime, coupled with Haywood's family history, afforded abundant proof of insanity. Dr Cuthbert Stanislaw Morrison, the superintendent of the Hereford City and County Lunatic Asylum, had been asked to examine Haywood and prepare a report on his mental condition. Morrison categorised Haywood as 'an imbecile of the higher grade', describing the murder as 'of a peculiarly ferocious and cruel character commonly observed in alcoholic homicide.' Morrison theorised that inherited mental instability and feebleness of the mind, in conjunction with alcoholic intoxication, had led Haywood to a sudden explosive impulse, possibly after receiving some 'trifling provocation' from his wife. In Morrison's opinion, Haywood's mind was so affected that, at the time of the murder, he was incapable of knowing the nature and quality of his act or of realising that such an act was wrong.

However, Morrison's views were largely negated by Dr J. Oswald Lane, the medical officer at Hereford Prison. Haywood had been under Dr Lane's care since he was first incarcerated in July and the doctor told the court that the prisoner's conduct to date had been good and that absolutely no manifestations of insanity had been observed.

It was left to Mr Justice Bigham to clarify matters for the jury. He advised them not to trouble their minds with the conflicting medical opinions but to instead use their common sense to answer one simple question – at the time of the crime, did the prisoner appreciate that what he was doing was wrong?

Lunatics, said Bigham, did not escape punishment for crimes if they were conscious of their wrongdoing. Yet, if Haywood was not aware that he was doing wrong when he killed his wife then he ought to be acquitted. Bigham reminded the jury that, both before and after the crime, Haywood had been seen and spoken to by several witnesses, all of whom testified that he was acting and speaking as if he was fully conscious of his deeds and words. He was doubtless drunk at the time of the killing but intoxication was no excuse for crime. The jury should bear in mind that Haywood had fabricated an explanation for the death of his wife and that he must have had his story ready very soon after the crime was committed since, at lunchtime on the day of his wife's death, he was already telling people that she had met with an accident and giving details of how that accident occurred.

The defence had intimated that the very ferocity of the crime was indicative of the perpetrator's insanity. However the enormity of the crime could not really be used in the prisoner's defence, otherwise the greater the crime, the better the culprit's chance of escaping punishment.

The jury retired for only a few minutes before returning with a verdict of 'Guilty' and, remarking that he believed that the jury had come to the proper conclusion, Mr Justice Bigham pronounced the death sentence.

William Haywood was executed at Hereford Prison on 15 December 1903 by Henry Pierrepoint, who was assisted by John Ellis. According to prison chaplain Revd C.A. Treherne, Haywood died truly penitent, acknowledging the justice of his sentence. In preparing for the execution, prison officials noticed that repairs were being carried out to the chimney of the Merton Hotel, which stood directly opposite the prison. Scaffolding erected by the builders afforded an excellent view over the high walls of the prison to the place of execution. On hearing this, the Under Sheriff of Herefordshire approached the proprietors of Messrs Lewis & Son, Builders, and asked them to refrain from using the scaffolding during the execution, offering to pay them for any time lost as a consequence. The builders agreed and, on the morning of the execution, a police guard was placed at the foot of the ladders leading to the scaffold to prevent any spectators from trying to secure an uninterrupted view of the proceedings.

Ironically, at the funeral of Jane Haywood, held at St Leonard's Church in Yarpole, an elaborate floral wreath was placed on the coffin. It bore the inscription 'With fondest love from her dear children and ever-loving husband.'

18

'YOU MUST HAVE HAD AN AWFUL NIGHT HERE'

Eye, 1912

On 26 February 1912, two police constables were on duty in the crowded Central Hall at the House of Commons when their attention was drawn to a man who appeared to be behaving strangely. Before the officers could approach the man, he suddenly produced a revolver and fired it over the heads of the crowd at the ceiling.

Courageously, the two constables tackled the shooter, tightly grasping his wrists and forcing his hands downwards. Hearing the shot, Chief Inspector Scantlebury rushed to assist his men and between them, the three officers managed to subdue the man who was struggling violently and shouting, 'Messiah. Tolstoy. Gentlemen, down tools.'

When the man was finally disarmed, his revolver was found to contain one blank cartridge and four ball cartridges, with a further ten cartridges in the pocket of his overcoat, along with some phenacetin tablets prescribed for headaches.

Taken to the police station at Cannon Row, the man gave his name as Revd Samuel Henry and told the police that he was a licensed preacher of Moreton Lodge, at Eye in Herefordshire. He was charged with wantonly discharging a firearm to the common danger in a public place and appeared before magistrates at Bow Street Police Court on 27 February.

Chief Inspector Scantlebury was called to give his account of the events in the House, most of which were disputed by Revd Henry. Henry denied struggling with the police officers, saying that after firing the revolver he had pointed the gun at the floor to avoid injuring them and surrendered quietly. There was no necessity for the police to have employed such violent tactics in detaining him, said Henry, adding that if such force was used against 'an accredited priest who had led a blameless life' then he dreaded to think what sort of treatment was meted out to criminals. Henry told the magistrate that he was sure that Scantlebury was a very nice fellow and that he was pleased to have met him but the officer had certainly made a mistake with his testimony.

It emerged that Henry was the author of a great many Socialist pamphlets and a book entitled 'Tolstoi and The Messiah' [*sic*]. Henry believed that the government had suppressed his book and had gone to the House to bring attention to the fact that he was being silenced. In advance of his visit, he had sent a telegram to Prime Minister Mr Asquith and also contacted the press but had received no response to either approach.

It was obvious that Henry saw nothing wrong in his actions. He asked Scantlebury if anyone had been terrified or incapacitated from service, or if anyone had suffered 'broken down nerves' as a result of the incident. When Scantlebury admitted that nobody had, Henry said, 'I am very pleased to hear that,' as though a lack of physical and psychological harm to the innocent bystanders had somehow justified his means of protest. There was nothing dangerous, offensive or alarming about the trivial matter of firing a revolver into the air, said Henry, insisting that the action was simply a straightforward method of drawing attention to a fact.

Magistrate Mr Marsham seemed at a loss as to how to deal with Henry, eventually remanding him in custody and telling him that he would arrange for him to be examined by the prison doctor.

'What do you mean by a doctor?' queried Henry. 'I could make out any man I choose to be insane. If you, Sir, were being watched, it would not take them long to come to a verdict.'

'I hope not,' commented the magistrate drily, signalling that Henry should be removed from court.

The findings of the prison doctor into Henry's mental state are not recorded but Henry seemed to have escaped lightly as he was soon back at his Herefordshire home, which he shared with his wife and their five

The Right Honorable Mr Asquith KC MP, later Prime Minister. (Author's collection)

children, aged between ten months and eight years. Moreton Lodge was also home to a seventeen-year-old maid, Fanny Brown, who had worked for the family for more than a year.

On the morning of 11 April, Revd and Mrs Henry played golf together, returning to the house in time for lunch. Revd Henry then went for a walk alone until teatime and the family spent the evening together, before Mrs Henry retired to bed at about half-past nine, taking with her a cup of tea and a couple of slices of bread and butter. According to Fanny Brown, it was just another normal day, although she did think that her mistress seemed a little worried about something.

Fanny went to bed at about ten o'clock, in the room she shared with two of the children, after bidding 'goodnight' to Revd Henry, who was writing at the dining room table. At about half-past eleven, Fanny heard Revd Henry going to bed. He first stopped briefly at his wife's bedroom before proceeding to his own bedroom, which he shared with his son. What Fanny heard next was enough to make her blood run cold.

A terrible screeching, gurgling sound came from Mrs Henry's bedroom and, seconds later, Revd Henry ran from his own room into that of his wife. All was quiet for a few moments then Revd Henry burst into Fanny's bedroom without knocking.

'Fanny, for heaven's sake be quiet. The mistress has cut her throat,' Henry told the terrified maid. He asked her if he might bring the baby into her and naturally Fanny agreed. The infant, who slept with her mother, was covered in blood from head to foot and Fanny quickly found some clean clothes for her and put her to sleep in her own bed.

Revd Henry moved his other daughter, who also shared her mother's bedroom, into his own room before returning to Fanny's bedroom.

'Should I go for help?' Fanny asked him but Henry insisted that his wife was beyond any help.

'Wait until morning and then I will go into Leominster for the policeman,' he told her. He then removed his trousers, jacket and waistcoat and curled up at the foot of Fanny's bed, pulling the counterpane over himself.

Not surprisingly, Fanny spent a sleepless night, sharing her double bed with a half-naked man, a baby and two small children and knowing that there was a dead body in the house. At five o'clock, Revd Henry woke up and announced his intention of going to Leominster. Having washed, shaved and dressed, he then demanded his breakfast before going.

By now, Fanny was beginning to despair. She briefly excused herself and, carrying the baby, rushed to the neighbours Mr and Mrs Conod. Thrusting the baby at them, she quickly explained what had happened before rushing back to Moreton Lodge to prepare her master's breakfast, which he asked her to serve in his study upstairs.

While he was eating, another neighbour, Mary Edwards, called at the house. Having heard of the events of the previous night from Mr and Mrs Conod, she decided to see if she could help in any way. Fanny called upstairs to announce Mary Edwards' arrival and Revd Henry met her on the landing.

Mary asked him if there was anything she could do for Mrs Henry but Revd Henry assured her that his wife was quite dead. Nevertheless, Mary went into Mrs Henry's bedroom to see for herself, touching Mrs Henry and finding her stone cold.

'You must have had an awful night here,' she commented to Revd Henry, who had waited for her on the landing.

'We have had rather,' agreed Henry, adding, 'Death is bad in any form but in this case it is worse.'

After Mary Edwards had left the house and Revd Henry had finished eating, Fanny asked him if he had enjoyed his meal. 'Not very much,' he admitted, allowing her to clear his breakfast tray and take it back to the kitchen. Moments later, he followed her downstairs and picked up a cigarette, which he took back up to his study.

Suddenly, four shots rang out in rapid succession. Horrified, Fanny raced upstairs to the study, finding the door firmly locked. 'Master, what are you doing?' Fanny screamed through the locked door.

'It is all right, Fanny. Go for help,' Henry told her.

'Open the door,' Fanny said but Henry replied that he couldn't.

'Where are you?' asked Fanny. Henry told her that he was sitting in his chair. 'If you don't open the door, I shall go and do the same,' Fanny insisted and with that the door slowly swung open, allowing Fanny into the study. Henry had sat down again and was smoking his cigarette, a revolver resting in his lap and a slow trickle of blood running down one side of his face.

'Why did you do this?' Fanny asked Henry, who told her that he couldn't survive his wife. 'They will arrest me for what happened last night,' he said ruefully.

Fortunately for Fanny, the neighbour, Mr Conod, had grasped the urgency of the situation and had cycled as fast as he could to the police station at Leominster. PC Saunders was despatched to Moreton Lodge, arriving only two or three minutes after the frightened maid had managed to gain admittance to her master's study.

On arriving at the house, Saunders quickly assessed the scene and immediately called for back-up. Superintendent Charles Rooke collected Dr Robinson and drove to Moreton Lodge as quickly as possible, where they met Dr Thomas, who had already been summoned by Mr Conod and was in the process of bandaging Revd Henry's head. Between them, Rooke and Saunders carried Henry out to the police car and, with Thomas in attendance, Saunders drove him to Leominster Cottage Hospital. Meanwhile Rooke and Robinson went to Mrs Henry's bedroom.

Bertha Mary Henry lay dead on her bed, her nightclothes, bed linen and the bedroom floor soaked with blood. Her throat had been slashed so deeply that she was almost decapitated and there was also a small but deep cut on her right wrist. A closed, bloodstained razor lay on the bedside table. Although there was no sign that any struggle had taken place in the bedroom, Mrs Henry's nose appeared to have been pushed towards the left of her face, as if someone had exerted a great deal of pressure on it.

Rooke then moved from the bedroom to the study, where he took possession of Revd Henry's revolver. There were five discharged cartridges in the chamber and one live one. A search of the study revealed two bullet holes in the plaster of the walls and a third in the skirting board.

Revd Henry had been examined at the hospital and his injuries were not thought to be life-threatening. Rooke visited him at the hospital and charged him both with the wilful murder of his wife and with attempting to commit suicide by shooting himself.

'The first charge I had heard of at the hospital and it shocked me terribly. With regard to the second charge, as I already said to the police, it was only a toy revolver and I knew it would hardly kill anyone,' responded Henry.

The coroner for North Herefordshire, Mr C.E.A. Moore, opened an inquest into Bertha Henry's death at Eye on 17 April, at which the principal witness was Fanny Brown. Fanny revealed that she had purchased an *Exchange and Mart* magazine from Leominster and that Revd Henry had spotted an advertisement for a revolver in it. He had asked Fanny to write a letter to the advertiser and the gun was delivered to Leominster station, the parcel addressed to F. Brown, Moreton Lodge. Fanny signed for the parcel but had passed it straight to her master without even opening it.

'Did you ask him why he wanted the revolver?' Fanny was asked.

Fanny said she had and that Revd Henry had told her that he didn't like to be without a gun. She admitted that she had not mentioned the purchase of the weapon to Mrs Henry.

Fanny was then asked about the razor used to cut Mrs Henry's throat. She told the inquest that, after telling her that his wife was dead, Revd Henry had said that

The church at Eye. (© N. Sly)

he had taken the razor from his wife's hand and put it in his pocket. When Fanny served him breakfast the following morning, the razor was on his desk and Fanny said she had suggested that he replaced it in the bedroom.

Fanny was asked about her own breakfast and admitted to having eaten some bread and butter on the morning after Mrs Henry's death. She denied having drunk a glass of whisky and water but stated that Mr Henry had drunk some in her bedroom.

Although Fanny insisted that Revd and Mrs Henry appeared happy together, it emerged at the inquest that Revd Henry had recently lost his job and was being evicted from the house at the end of the month. He had applied for a job in Suffolk but had been unsuccessful and, as far as Fanny was aware, the family had no home to go to once they were turned out of Moreton Lodge. To add to the family's worries, Mrs Henry believed that she was pregnant again and had told Fanny that, if she was, she would commit suicide.

However, according to Dr Charles Robinson, Mrs Henry had definitely not committed suicide. The wound in her throat had bisected her Adam's apple – an extremely tough part of the throat. In addition, Robinson believed that there were actually two cuts across the front of Mrs Henry's throat, one running from right to left, the other from left to right. Both were deep cuts, as opposed to the rather tentative 'trial' cuts sometimes made by suicides. Finally, there was the question of the squashing pressure apparently applied to Mrs Henry's nose.

Although Revd Henry vigorously denied any responsibility for his wife's death, in his summary for the inquest jury the coroner pointed out that there was little doubt that Bertha Henry had met her death in Moreton Lodge at a time when, apart from the deceased herself, there were only two adults present in the house.

There was no evidence of any stranger having entered the house and Dr Robinson had categorically stated that Mrs Henry could not have committed suicide hence there were only two possible suspects – Fanny Brown and Revd Henry. The killing had been committed with Revd Henry's own razor and, according to Fanny Brown, had occurred immediately after she heard her master come upstairs. Therefore, it seemed as though Revd Henry was the only person who could possibly have killed his wife.

The jury needed only ten minutes deliberation to reach the same conclusions, returning with a verdict of wilful murder against Revd Samuel Henry.

By the conclusion of the inquest, Revd Samuel Henry had already appeared before magistrates and been remanded in custody and it was fully expected that he would stand trial for the murder of his wife. However, on 9 May 1920, there was a further sitting of the magistrates at Leominster Police Court, at which it was agreed that the charge of wilful murder against him should be struck out. It transpired that Revd Henry had been under the care of a doctor for mental health problems for some time and, since his incarceration, following his release from hospital after the death of his wife and his own attempted suicide, his condition had worsened considerably.

Initially, he had become very depressed and had refused food. Gradually his behaviour became wild and erratic and he was placed in a padded cell for his own

Bertha Mary Henry's grave at Eye. (© N. Sly)

safety. Eventually, he was removed to an asylum, from where his condition was reported to be 'very, very bad indeed.' It was agreed that all charges against him would be placed on hold and in the event of his recovery a new warrant would be issued for his arrest.

The author has been unable to find a record of Revd Samuel Henry ever facing further charges pertaining to the death of his wife. However in 1925, the death of a Samuel Henry, aged fifty-one, is recorded in Berkshire, which would coincide with the registration district for the Broadmoor Criminal Lunatic Asylum.

19

'EXCUSE MY FINGERS'

Hay-on-Wye, Herefordshire, 1921

Major Herbert Rowse Armstrong had practiced as a solicitor in the Herefordshire town of Hay-on-Wye for several years when, in 1921, he found himself in dispute with the town's other solicitors over the sale of an estate. Initially a junior partner with the firm Cheese and Armstrong, Armstrong had taken over the running of the practice after the senior partner and his wife died within a day of each other in 1914. Now, seven years later, he was being pressured by fellow solicitor, Oswald Norman Martin, to complete on the sale of a property, for which Armstrong held a deposit of £500 from Martin's client.

Given the dispute between the two men, it came as a complete surprise to Oswald Martin when, on 20 September 1921, he received an unexpected gift from Armstrong in the form of a box of chocolates, which were delivered to his house. As neither Martin nor his wife, Constance, were particularly fond of sweets, they each ate only one chocolate before putting the box away, to be brought out on 8 October after a dinner party.

Much to Constance Martin's embarrassment, one of her dinner guests reported being violently ill on the day after the get together. Dorothy Martin – the wife of Oswald's brother, Gilbert – was the only guest to have partaken of the chocolates after the meal, although this fact wasn't noted at the time.

With the property deal still stalling, Oswald Martin's client finally felt that enough was enough and decided to withdraw from the transaction completely. When Martin communicated his client's instructions to Armstrong, it was suggested by Armstrong that the two solicitors should meet to thrash out the deal between them. Accordingly, on 26 October 1921, Martin presented himself at Armstrong's house, 'Mayfield', having been invited for afternoon tea.

The host poured tea and handed his guest a buttered scone, using his fingers rather than proffering the plate. 'Excuse my fingers,' he asked Martin. Within a short time of returning home, Martin found himself inexplicably stricken by a mysterious illness. Throughout that night, he vomited persistently, his heart raced and he had stomach pains and attacks of diarrhoea. When he awoke the next morning, he found himself extremely sensitive to light.

On hearing of Martin's illness, Herbert Armstrong seemed most concerned, offering to help with his fellow solicitor's work during Martin's enforced absence from the office.

Martin's wife, Constance, was the daughter of John Davies, the chemist in Hay-on-Wye. On hearing of his son-in-law's illness and of the similar symptoms suffered by Dorothy Martin after eating a chocolate gifted to the Martins by Armstrong, Davies realised that Armstrong had frequently purchased arsenic from his shop over the preceding few months, saying that he wanted to make up a weed-killing solution to deal with the dandelions in his lawn at home.

Davies put his suspicions to the doctor treating his son-in-law and Dr Hincks accordingly collected samples of Oswald Martin's vomit and urine, sending them with the remains of the box of chocolates to the Clinical Research Association in London. When tested, all were found to contain arsenic.

The police were notified and immediately began a discreet investigation into Armstrong's conduct. Major Armstrong, a prominent freemason and member of the Conservative Party, was a highly respected solicitor in Hay and his character was hitherto without blemish, hence the police enquiries were conducted in complete secrecy. Unaware that he was under investigation, Armstrong continued to issue invitations to Martin to dine with him, which Martin persistently declined, all the while trying not to alert Armstrong to the fact that he was under suspicion.

By 31 December 1921, the police had gathered sufficient evidence against Armstrong to pounce and he was arrested in his Broad Street office and charged with the attempted murder of Oswald Martin. However, the charge of attempted murder was little more than a holding charge as, during their investigations, the police had developed strong suspicions that Armstrong had been responsible for the death of his wife, Katherine, on 22 February 1921.

Herbert and Katherine Armstrong had been married since 1907 and had three children. Always a rather sickly woman, with a tendency towards hypochondria, Katherine Armstrong had begun to suffer from gastric illness in May 1920, shortly after making a new will. In her previous will, the majority of her estate had been divided between her children, with her husband benefiting only from an annual legacy of just £50. Now, according to the terms of her new will, Katherine's estate was left to her husband in its entirety.

By 22 August 1920, Katherine Armstrong's sickliness had progressed to a real illness and she was admitted to the Barnwood Hospital for Mental Disorders in Gloucester. On admission, having been certified as insane by a Justice of the Peace, doctors found her to have a heart murmur, as well as being confused and delusional. Between 5 October and 4 November, Mrs Armstrong was treated with a medicine containing four minims of arsenic in solution, which equated to a dose

Broad Street, Hay-on-Wye, 1960s. (Author's collection)

of three twentieths of a grain of arsenic per day. This treatment was discontinued after 4 November.

Armstrong appeared to show the greatest concern for his wife's wellbeing, visiting her as often as the doctors would allow him to and, by mid-January 1921, he was keen that she should be allowed home. Her delusions now very much a thing of the past, Katherine was released from hospital on 22 January to find that her husband had engaged the services of a nurse to look after her. Yet Katherine was obviously still far from well and the nurse, Muriel Kinsey, was to hand in her notice just a few days later, claiming that she was unable to cope with her patient's threats of suicide. Katherine refused to take anything but her own homeopathic medicine, claiming that the doctors in the asylum had 'poisoned her with drugs'. She also frequently asked about the likely effects of throwing herself out of an upstairs window. On 27 January, Muriel Kinsey was replaced by nurse Eva Allen.

For the following few weeks, Katherine Armstrong suffered repeated attacks of vomiting, coupled with muscular spasms and, on 22 February, she finally died, just two weeks after her forty-eighth birthday. For the few days prior to her death, she was so weak that she could not get out of bed and had lost the use of her hands, legs and feet, having to be hand-fed by her nurse. The cause of her death was given as heart disease (one year), nephritis (six months) and acute gastritis (twenty-one days).

Armstrong was hardly the grieving husband. He immediately took a month's holiday abroad and, on returning to Hay, proposed marriage to a long-term acquaintance, Mrs Marion Gale. He had met Mrs Gale in 1915, while stationed at Bournemouth during his wartime service with the Royal Engineers.

On Armstrong's arrest for the attempted murder of Oswald Martin, he was searched and found to have a small packet containing one twentieth of an ounce of arsenic in his jacket pocket. Yet more of the poison was found in the drawers of his desk and his assertion that he had purchased it for killing dandelions was not believed. On 2 January 1922, Katherine Armstrong's body was exhumed from the churchyard at nearby Cusop and Home Office pathologist Sir Bernard Spilsbury conducted a post-mortem examination on her remains. On testing, her organs were found to contain three-and-three-quarters grains of arsenic. Her husband was formally charged with her murder on 19 January 1922.

Armstrong then faced the undoubtedly personally humiliating experience of appearing before the very magistrates to whom he had previously acted in a professional capacity as clerk. There, the presiding magistrate, Mr W. Mortimer Baylis, heard from numerous witnesses about the gradual deterioration of Katherine Armstrong's health leading to her eventual death. One witness in particular caused a buzz of interest in the packed courtroom – a mysterious veiled woman, known only to the court as 'Mrs X'.

Although her identity was ultimately revealed to be Mrs Marion Gale, as far as the magistrates' court was concerned, the woman remained incognito. A widow, she described her first meeting with the defendant in the autumn of 1915, when she told the court that she knew that he was married, although she had never met Mrs Armstrong. She had dined with Armstrong in London in 1920 and the couple had resumed their friendship after Mrs Armstrong's death in 1921. At that time, 'Mrs X' had been invited to stay at Armstrong's home and Armstrong had proposed marriage. 'I was considering it,' Mrs X told the court. Although she was not cross-examined, she was asked by Mr Micklethwait, Armstrong's defending solicitor, if she was aware that Armstrong had also proposed to another woman. 'I have no knowledge of that,' she replied.

While Armstrong was remanded in custody awaiting his trial, his three children and two of his servants were staying with a family friend in Hereford. It was reported on 11 February that the friend had received a box of chocolates doctored with tintacks and that police were investigating the matter.

Armstrong was eventually committed for trial at the Hereford Assizes before Mr Justice Darling, who stated that it might be necessary to hold a Special Assize solely for the purpose of hearing Armstrong's case. However, even before the case could come to trial, Armstrong's solicitors issued a writ for contempt of court against the *Daily Express* newspaper, which, in the course of their coverage of proceedings at the magistrates' court, had published a sketch purporting to be of Armstrong's eyes, describing him as '...the man with the harassed face and despondent attitudes.'

It was the contention of Armstrong's legal representatives that the article and picture published by the newspaper were prejudicial to their client receiving a fair trial. At the High Court of Justice, the Lord Chief Justice, Mr Justice Shearman and Mr Justice Roche agreed that the article in question had been in dubious taste but did not believe that it had prejudiced a fair hearing for the accused.

Thus Armstrong's trial opened at Hereford on 3 April 1922 and was to last for ten days. (The early days of the trial were marked by a fierce snowstorm both outside and inside the court, as snow blew unchecked through an open window.) Ernest Pollock prosecuted the case, with Sir Henry Curtis Bennett defending Armstrong, who was charged with the murder of his wife and the attempted murder of Mr Oswald Martin. In the judge's opinion, there was insufficient evidence to charge him with sending poisoned chocolates to Martin, so that charge was dropped and Armstrong pleaded 'Not Guilty' to the remaining two indictments.

One of the major issues at the trial was the question of whether or not Katherine Armstrong had actually wanted to die. Her first nurse, Muriel Kinsey, had left within days of taking up her appointment because she felt that Mrs Armstrong was suicidal. However her replacement, Nurse Allen, told the court that Mrs Armstrong had asked her, 'I am not going to die, am I, nurse? Because I have everything to live for, my children and my husband.'

Liverpool solicitor Arthur Edward Chevalier told the court that, in August 1920, he had cause to visit Mrs Armstrong at her home and, at that time, had formed the opinion that she was suicidal. He had recommended to Major Armstrong that his razor should be removed from the room as a precaution, which Armstrong immediately did, also removing a revolver at the same time.

It was also noted that Mrs Armstrong was a devotee of homeopathic medicine and that Nurse Allen was aware that she had two bottles in a cupboard at the end of the bed, one containing *nux vomica* and another mixture, the name of which Nurse Allen was unable to recall. However, given Mrs Armstrong's debilitated state, there was doubt as to whether or not she would have been able to reach the bottles. Pollock, for the prosecution, insisted that Mrs Armstrong had been given a fatal dose of arsenic in the twenty-four hours before her death and, as her physical condition at the time would have prevented her from taking the medicine herself, then she must have been poisoned. Her husband alone had the means, motive and opportunity. By process of elimination, Major Armstrong was the only person with access to his wife both in August 1920, when she was first taken ill, and immediately before her death.

The defence countered with the assertion that, while they did not dispute the cause of death as arsenical poisoning, they denied that Major Armstrong had been the person who administered the poison.

The mysterious 'Mrs X' testified again and although she was not veiled as she had been during her appearance before the magistrates, her identity was still concealed and the press were forbidden to take any photographs of her. Once again, she stated that she had always been aware that Armstrong was a married man with children and that, until the death of his wife, he had been just a family friend to her.

The court also heard from two gardeners employed by Major Armstrong, both of whom testified that his garden was 'a terrible place for weeds'. Neither gardener had ever seen Major Armstrong using weedkiller on the garden himself, but one, Mr Jay, remembered Armstrong showing him a patch of garden where he had used weedkiller that he had mixed himself. There had been some argument in court about the fact that Major Armstrong had bought arsenic to use for killing weeds in the winter. Mr Jay gave his professional opinion that it was better to kill weeds in January than in June, since the wet ground absorbed the weedkiller and made it more effective. Both gardeners stated that they had used weedkiller themselves in the Armstrongs' garden.

The court then heard from Dr Hincks who had treated both Mrs Armstrong and Mr Martin throughout their respective illnesses. Hincks stated that, when Mrs Armstrong was initially taken ill, he had been of the opinion that she had been poisoned but that there had been nothing about her condition that was inconsistent with natural illness. He discussed autointoxication, informing the court that the body could poison itself, for example with decayed teeth or even just general illness.

Referring to Mr Martin, he told the court that he had treated the solicitor with a bismuth mixture that had contained no arsenic whatsoever. When chemist John Davies was called to the stand, he testified to having supplied Major Armstrong with white arsenic, stating that Armstrong had told him that he wanted the poison to make weedkiller and that he had signed the poisons register at every purchase. Davies admitted that, given the size of Armstrong's garden, at the time he hadn't considered the amount of arsenic purchased by the solicitor excessive.

Davies told the court that white arsenic was routinely coloured with charcoal before being sold. However, a packet of uncoloured arsenic bearing Davies's shop label was produced in court, much to Davies's surprise. His assistant, John Hird, was then questioned at length about selling poison to Armstrong in January 1921, with particular attention paid to the way the arsenic had been wrapped and whether or not it had been coloured with charcoal, as demanded by the law.

Sergeant Worthing testified to finding poison at Armstrong's house and also to finding a recipe for weedkiller, which used half a pound of white arsenic and half a pound of caustic soda to a gallon of water. The ingredients were then boiled until the mixture was clear, after which one teacupful of the mixture was used in a gallon of water to treat weeds. Both Sergeant Worthing and Chief Inspector Crutchett of Scotland Yard stated that Armstrong had cooperated fully in their investigations and had at no time objected to a search of his home or office being made.

Oswald Martin had already testified about his illness and the persistence of Major Armstrong in inviting him for tea. Now the court heard from the medical witnesses. Sir Bernard Spilsbury concluded that Mrs Armstrong had clearly died from arsenical poisoning and that large doses of the poison had been administered to her throughout the last week of her life, culminating in a fatal dose within twenty-four hours of her death. Mr John Webster, pathological chemist to the Home Office and Sir William Wilcox, the Home Office medical adviser, both supported Spilsbury's evidence. According to the experts, this pattern was inconsistent with suicide, since a person intent on suicide would be more likely to take one large dose of poison, two at most. Webster, described as 'a nervous little man in a large frock coat', told the court that the amount of arsenic found in Mrs Armstrong's remains was the largest amount he personally had ever found in a body. However, he did concede that, although he would expect two grains of arsenic to be a fatal dose, he was aware of people taking up to fifteen grains and surviving. Once the medical witnesses had testified, the prosecution rested.

In a speech lasting for more than two hours, counsel for the defence, Sir Henry Curtis Bennett, then proceeded to attack every aspect of the case outlined by the prosecution. He pointed out that Mrs Armstrong had been in poor health prior to the alleged first attempt at poisoning her in August 1920, already displaying many of the symptoms that had since been attributed to her ingestion of arsenic.

Major Armstrong was a loving husband to her and the couple lived on affectionate terms. Anyone in the Armstrong household – including Katherine Armstrong herself – could have administered the poison, said Bennett, and his client had no motive for so doing.

There was no question in anybody's mind that as soon as Mrs Armstrong was admitted to hospital, her condition began to improve. Surely, said Sir Henry, if she had been suffering from arsenical poisoning, then the administration of a tonic containing yet more arsenic would have precluded any improvement in her health?

Bennett argued that the facts of the case pointed to suicide by Katherine Armstrong. He reminded the court of the affectionate relationship between Armstrong and his wife, suggesting that all the evidence that had been heard indicated that Katherine had received a large, fatal dose of arsenic on 16 February and that it had been self-administered.

He stated that there was nothing to suggest that Mrs Armstrong's second will was not her own work and ridiculed a suggestion by the prosecution that Armstrong had wanted to get rid of his wife in order to marry another woman. With regard to Oswald Martin, Bennett maintained that there was nothing to suggest that he had suffered from arsenical poisoning apart from analysis of his samples and he reminded the jury that there was some question about the cleanliness of the bottles used to collect these samples, which had come from Mr Davies's shop. Even if Martin had been poisoned, there was absolutely no proof that it had been Armstrong's doing.

Why was the arsenic found on Major Armstrong on his arrest not coloured with charcoal, asked Bennett? And did it naturally follow that because Armstrong had poison about his person for killing weeds that he was intending to use it to poison somebody he didn't like? It made perfect sense for Armstrong to divide the arsenic he had bought into smaller packets to guard against the risk of spilling it or of it blowing away. 'No one with any common sense will ever buy arsenic for weed killing again,' said Bennett.

It was left to the judge to sum up the case but when the foreman of the jury was later interviewed by the press, he revealed that eleven of the twelve jurors had already reached their verdict before the judge had even commenced his summary. The jury failed to appreciate the defence counsel's argument that it was practical to divide the arsenic into small packets, finding it suspicious that Armstrong had split the poison into individual doses. Although the jury praised both counsels for the prosecution and defence for the way in which they handled the case, they had no hesitation in finding Major Armstrong guilty of the murder of his wife, leaving the judge to pronounce the death sentence upon him. Armstrong remained calm and collected as he heard the verdict. Finally Mr Justice Darling told the court that the matter of the attempted murder charge against the defendant could be left until the next Assizes.

An appeal was immediately instigated, which was heard before the Lord Chief Justice and Justices Avory and Shearman on 11 May 1922. Sir Henry Curtis Bennett continued to maintain that Mrs Armstrong had committed suicide, pointing out that there was absolutely no evidence to suggest that her husband had ever given her any food or drink containing poison.

Bennett then argued about significant dates in the case. Katherine Armstrong had been ill for several years with indigestion, neuritis and a loss of power in her hands and feet. On 4 August 1921, Mr Jay the gardener had bought ready-made weedkiller. Jay had sworn in court that he had personally used half a tin and that the remaining half tin was still in the shed after Major Armstrong's arrest.

On 22 August, Mrs Armstrong was admitted to Barnwood House hospital, at which point she was supposedly showing symptoms of arsenical poisoning. However, those symptoms could also apply to numerous other diseases. Arsenic administered in a tonic at the hospital should, at very least, have retarded her progress had she been poisoned with arsenic but on the contrary, while hospitalised she made a steady progress towards health.

Armstrong had purchased arsenic on 11 January 1922 and his wife had returned home on 22 January. When she again fell ill on 6 February, Armstrong himself sent for the doctor, telling him, 'My wife is not so well and I want you to keep an eye on her.' Nurse Kinsey had quickly left the Armstrongs' employ because she believed that Katherine Armstrong was suicidal.

Stating that Major Armstrong's behaviour throughout was more indicative of innocence than of guilt, Sir Henry went on to say that it was his belief that the prosecution had not satisfactorily proved the case against Armstrong.

The Court of Appeal failed to agree and Armstrong's appeal was dismissed. He was hanged by John Ellis at Gloucester Prison on 31 May 1922.

It was later suggested that Armstrong might even have been responsible for yet another suspicious death in Hay-on-Wye. In October 1921, estate agent William Davies died suddenly and unexpectedly – like Oswald Martin, he too was in dispute with Major Armstrong. Yet, in more recent years, questions have been asked about the possible involvement of Oswald Martin and his father-in-law, chemist John Davies, in Mrs Armstrong's death. It has been theorised that Davies – aware that Mrs Armstrong was suicidal and would have access to the arsenic that her husband had purchased from his shop to kill weeds – may have framed Armstrong for her murder, in order to ensure that his son-in-law's was the most prominent and successful solicitor's practice in the area by eliminating Martin's only real business competitor.

Regardless of any conspiracy theories, Herbert Rowse Armstrong went to his death still strongly protesting his innocence, in spite of an offer of £5,000 by a contemporary newspaper for a last-minute confession of guilt.

20

'TAKE THAT HORRID MAN AWAY!'

Pembridge, 1922

Twelve-year-old Evan Hicks normally lived in the orphanage at Leominster. However, over Christmas 1922, he was staying with his grandparents, Samuel and Mary Brown, at their home in Bridge Street, Pembridge. On 29 December, Evan was playing outside when he saw a man walking through the village from the direction of the station towards the cottage next door to his grandparents' home, where Mrs Wilhelmina Sainsbury lived with her adopted daughter, Winifred Buckeridge, and her granddaughter, Hilda.

The man was smiling pleasantly as he walked up the steps outside the cottage and knocked on the door. When the door was opened, Evan heard the man say 'Good afternoon' to whoever had answered it, before being invited inside.

Mary Brown was upstairs in her cottage at the time and, through her bedroom window, she too saw the smiling man approaching the house and being admitted. A few minutes later, Mrs Brown decided to check on Evan and went to her own front door. As she stood chatting to the boy on her doorstep, they suddenly heard two loud bangs coming from Mrs Sainsbury's home. Moments later, Mrs Sainsbury flung open her front door and shouted 'Murder!' at the top of her voice. 'Will someone go for the police?' she continued, 'This man is shooting us all.'

'What man?' asked Mrs Brown, at which Mrs Sainsbury pointed upstairs.

Mary Brown told her grandson to run for the village policeman, who lived less than 20 yards from Mrs Sainsbury's cottage. She then closed her front door and ran through her home, out of the back door and across the back gardens to the house of Miss Russell, who was Mrs Sainsbury's neighbour on the other side, telling her, 'There is a man shooting people next door.'

Bridge Street, Pembridge. The timbered, brick house on the left was Mrs Sainsbury's cottage. (© N. Sly)

Pembridge. (© N. Sly)

Miss Russell and Mrs Brown ran out into the street where they saw labourer George Henry Powell walking towards them. Miss Russell rushed to tell him what was happening and Powell bravely went to Mrs Sainsbury's aid.

As he approached her cottage, he heard a loud bang from inside. The front door of the cottage was slightly ajar and Powell gave it a push. As it swung open, he saw Mrs Sainsbury slowly falling to the floor and, at almost the same time, Powell registered the presence of a man in the room, a revolver held in his right hand.

'Hello, young man,' the man said pleasantly, walking towards George Powell, who was standing on the doorstep in a state of shock, trying to make up his mind whether or not the man was intending to shoot him and if he should stand his ground or run away. As Powell slowly backed down the steps outside Mrs Sainsbury's cottage, he saw the man step over her body and follow him outside. As he reached the road, the man threw his gun down with such force that it flew clear across the street and hit a wall on the other side. Powell ran over and picked it up. The man then undid his belt, on which there was a holster for the revolver as well as an ammunition pouch, and tossed it onto the ground.

By that time the local policeman, PC Joseph Prosser, had arrived on the scene. He quickly arrested the man and took him back inside the cottage. The obviously dead body of Mrs Sainsbury lay close to the front door and, as Prosser put on the handcuffs, the man snatched up some clothes and threw them over Mrs Sainsbury's head. 'Oh, dear! This is all through her,' he said, then told Prosser, 'Go and see what you can do upstairs.'

Prosser could hear groaning coming from upstairs, along with the unmistakeable sound of a sobbing child. Taking the man by the collar and frog-marching him upstairs, Prosser went into the bedroom where he found a woman lying on the bed with her arm around a little girl, who was clutching her mother desperately around her neck. At the sight of the policeman and his charge, the child became hysterical, screaming 'Take that horrid man away!' and 'Don't let that bad man hurt Mamma.'

Mrs Russell, a trained nurse who now ran the village post office, had come to the cottage to see if she could be of assistance. She arrived minutes before the village doctor, Dr T. Beardmore Gornall. Gornall managed to pry the screaming child from her mother and passed her to Mrs Russell, telling her to take her outside. He then turned his attention to the injured woman.

She was twenty-eight-year-old Winifred Buckeridge and, in spite of having been shot in the chest at close range she was still alive, although obviously in a critical condition. Deathly pale and breathing in fast, shallow gasps, Winifred repeatedly asked the doctor, 'Shall I die?' and implored him, 'Look after baby,' referring to four-year-old Hilda.

As Gornall cut away her clothes in order to better examine her chest, the woman groaned in pain. 'Shall I get better?' she persisted, adding that she wanted to get better because of her baby. Twice she enquired about her mother and asked where 'baby' was, but on no occasion did she make any reference to how her wounds had been caused.

Gornall found two wounds on Winifred's chest. On the left-hand side was a small, round wound, roughly the size of an old sixpence, which was covered with a piece of cottonwool. 'I put that in,' said Winifred, when the doctor asked her about the cottonwool. The second wound was located on the other side of Winifred's chest, on the outside of her right breast. This wound was covered by a piece of grey wool and, when the doctor removed the wool, he found a bullet located beneath it. He surmised that Winifred Buckeridge had been shot, the bullet entering the left side of her chest and exiting on the right.

Meanwhile, the handcuffed man was sitting on the bedroom floor, an interested spectator to the doctor's attempts to help Mrs Buckeridge. PC Prosser pulled him to his feet and searched him, putting the contents of the man's pockets into a handkerchief which he then tied into a little bundle. Prosser eventually led the man downstairs and sat him in a chair in the kitchen, where he cautioned him and charged him with the wilful murder of Mrs Sainsbury. Initially the man made no reply to the charge but then buried his head in his hands and said, 'Oh, dear, this will kill my poor mother.' He then asked if the injured woman upstairs wanted to say anything to him.

Up in the bedroom, Gornall urged Winifred to lie still and not to try and talk. He asked somebody to fetch hot water bottles and put them against her feet, then dressed her wounds with gauze and gave her a painkilling injection of morphine. By now, a second doctor, Dr Milner, had arrived from Kington to assist Gornall, along with the Kington policeman, PC Meredith. As soon as his colleague arrived, PC Prosser arranged for his prisoner to be taken by car to Kington police station.

Together, the two doctors worked on Mrs Buckeridge until her condition improved slightly, at which time Milner left. Gornall arranged for a nurse from Leominster to come in and care for her and, while awaiting Nurse Brace's arrival, he brought in a neighbour, Mrs Newman, to sit with the wounded woman. When he explained to Winifred Buckeridge that he was leaving, she began to panic. 'Will that man come at me again?' she asked the doctor, who reassured her that she was safe.

Gornall called on Mrs Buckeridge again later that evening, finding her condition to be unchanged since he had left her. He went back to the cottage at about half-past five the following morning to find Nurse Brace bending over her patient. 'I think she has just died,' the nurse told Gornall.

Post-mortem examinations conducted on Mrs Sainsbury and Mrs Buckeridge showed that both women had been shot. Mrs Sainsbury had been shot three times, once in her chest, with the bullet exiting her back, once just below her left shoulderblade and once in her groin, with the bullet exiting through her right buttock. Mrs Sainsbury had bled to death, as had Mrs Buckeridge, although the younger woman's bleeding had been largely internal.

The man under arrest for the wilful murder of Mrs Sainsbury was immediately additionally charged with the wilful murder of Mrs Buckeridge. He was thirty-three-year-old George Vincent Buckeridge, Winifred Buckeridge's estranged husband and the father of little Hilda.

George and Winifred had married in 1915. They had undergone two wedding ceremonies, the first at Hereford registry office and the second at the Roman Catholic church in Hereford, since George was a Roman Catholic and his mother was very keen for her son's bride to adopt that faith. In June 1916, George was called up to serve in the Army and saw active service in France. While he was away, his new wife divided her time between living with her mother and staying in Hereford with her mother-in-law.

The couple's daughter, Hilda, was born in 1918 but by the time George was discharged from the Army in 1919, his marriage had all but ended and, before long, Winifred left him. George was absolutely devastated. He was deeply in love with his wife and, after she left, he could not eat or sleep and spent hours just sitting brooding about what might have been. His mother, with whom he was now living, urged him to try and snap out of his depression but there was no consoling George, who told her, 'If this keeps up, I shall be in an asylum. I cannot stand it.'

Eventually, he seemed to pull himself together and, in 1920, went off to work in Nuneaton. He followed this employment with a job in Sleaford and his mother didn't see him from March 1922 until he returned home for Christmas that year. At that time, Mrs Buckeridge senior was horrified by her son's appearance. He had lost a lot of weight and was suffering badly from his nerves. He was also complaining of excruciatingly painful headaches and taking strychnine, which he told his mother had been prescribed for his nerves.

George spent a miserable Christmas, refusing to join in with any of the festivities and preferring to stay in the kitchen alone. On 26 December he went for a long walk, returning in a highly agitated state, his face flushed and his hands trembling violently. He refused any food and left his mother's house later that afternoon, carrying his suitcase.

George returned to his mother's house the following evening, when she described him as being 'as white as death'. He left again the next morning, having drunk a cup of tea but eaten nothing, telling his mother that he was going to Derby on his way to work.

In fact, George Buckeridge had visited Pembridge on the night of 26 December, calling at the home of Mrs Elizabeth Lane. He arrived at about half-past ten at night and asked Mrs Lane if he might have a word with her in private. He was invited in and asked if Mrs Buckeridge was there. At this, Mrs Lane recognised him from a photograph that Winifred Buckeridge had once shown her and told him that she had not seen Winifred for more than six months.

Buckeridge explained that he was seeking evidence for a divorce and asked Mrs Lane if it were true that Winifred had almost parted her and her husband by 'carrying on' with Mr Lane. Mrs Lane admitted that this was the case but refused to explain further, saying that it was Winifred's lies and deceitfulness that had caused all the trouble between them. At this, George appeared sad but he left Mrs Lane's house without pressing her for further details.

Above & below: Two views of The New Inn, Pembridge. (© N. Sly)

Buckeridge then went to the New Inn, where he asked landlord James Evans for accommodation for the night. Buckeridge told Evans that his wife lived in Pembridge and that he had come to the village to look for evidence to obtain a divorce. Having stayed overnight, he left the next morning, returning at lunchtime for some bread and cheese and staying at the inn all afternoon before leaving again.

On the morning of 27 December, Buckeridge called in at the Queen's Head Hotel in Pembridge, where he met labourer Edward Victor Newman. After introducing himself to Newman, Buckeridge bought him a pint of beer and asked if he might have a private conversation with him. When Newman agreed, Buckeridge pulled a photograph of a woman out of his pocket and asked Newman if he recognised her.

'I do,' said Newman. 'I think she lives down Bridge Street and that her name is Mrs Buckeridge.'

Buckeridge asked Newman how well he knew the woman and Newman replied that he would pass the time of day with her but nothing more. Buckeridge then explained that he was the woman's husband and asked if she had been with anybody. Newman told Buckeridge that she had but refused to go into any more detail as he did not wish to interfere between man and wife.

Buckeridge told Newman that he was trying to get a divorce from his wife, although he was still very fond of her and had asked her numerous times to come back and live with him. 'I have tried in every way to control her,' he told Newman, adding that he had never really shown his wife how fond he was of her. At this point, Buckeridge put his head in his hands and began to sob.

Later that evening, Buckeridge went to visit PC Prosser, telling him that he was looking for evidence for a divorce. Prosser told him that it was against police regulations to interfere with divorce cases. Buckeridge told the constable that he had come from Nottingham and was about to catch the train back there, adding that the policeman would see him again. In fact, the next time Prosser saw Buckeridge was as he was leaving the cottage in Bridge Street, having just shot his wife and mother-in-law.

Buckeridge arrived back in Pembridge on the morning of 29 December and again called on Mrs Lane, telling her that he was tired and asking to rest. Mrs Lane thought that Buckeridge appeared sad and he was very quiet, although he told her that he had begged his wife to 'live a straightforward life' and that, if she came back to him, he was prepared to forgive her everything. He left Mrs Lane's house at about one o'clock and by half-past two he was back at the New Inn, asking if he could brush his boots. At three o'clock, he was seen by Edward Newman, from whom he asked directions to the home of a Mr Williams of Moseley. Newman pointed out the route and watched Buckeridge walk away.

When he arrived at Williams' house, Buckeridge asked his wife if he might speak to her husband. Emily Williams told him that he was at work, at which Buckeridge stood for some time without speaking before asking Mrs Williams if he might ask her one or two questions. When Mrs Williams agreed, Buckeridge began to question her about his wife's behaviour. Did she know Mrs Buckeridge? Had she ever seen her down around the meadows with men doing anything that was wrong?

Mrs Williams assured him that she hadn't, saying that she heard such a lot of rumours but took no notice of any of them. 'I think I have very good information all round and I am about wound up,' Buckeridge said, before asking Mrs Williams if she could direct him to the station. Mrs Williams escorted him to the nearest road and pointed out a stile that led to a shortcut. Mrs Williams was later to describe Buckeridge as looking 'mentally deranged', standing with one hand in his trouser pocket as if he were either deep in thought or his mind was wandering. Buckeridge called in to the New Inn again briefly later that afternoon for a cup of tea and by four o'clock was walking up the steps to the front door of his mother-in-law's cottage.

An inquest was opened into the deaths of the two women by Mr H.J. Southall, the coroner for North Hereford. Having heard from everyone who had encountered George Buckeridge in Pembridge before the murders, as well as evidence from PC Prosser and Dr Gornall, the coroner's jury returned a verdict of two counts of wilful murder against George Vincent Buckeridge, who was committed for trial at the next Hereford Assizes on the coroner's warrant.

The trial opened before Mr Justice Avory with Mr Bosanquet and Mr Rowland Powell prosecuting and Mr Graham Milward acting for the defence. Unusually for the period, there was one female juror who appeared thanks to the Sex Disqualification (Removal) Act of 1919, which permitted women to serve on juries for the first time. George Vincent Buckeridge was charged both with the murders of Wilhelmina Eliza Sainsbury and Winifred Buckeridge, pleading 'Not Guilty' to both charges.

The prosecution began by asking the judge if both indictments could be tried together. 'No, certainly not,' replied the judge, so Mr Bosanquet informed the court that he would be proceeding with the charge of wilful murder of Winifred Buckeridge. He suggested to the jury that the defence might well focus on their client's sanity at the time of the offence, telling them that the prosecution could find no evidence to show that Buckeridge was not in his right mind at the time the murder was committed.

The prosecution then called a series of witnesses from Pembridge to testify on the subject of Buckeridge's appearance in the village in the days preceding the shooting and his quest for evidence for a divorce from Winifred. Both George Powell and PC Prosser related their contact with Buckeridge in the immediate aftermath of the shootings, both saying that Buckeridge had seemed quite calm at the time and had only shown any real signs of agitation when he was handcuffed, when he suddenly seemed to appreciate what he had done.

Dr Gornall then took the stand to give his account of the day of the murders and of the injuries to both victims. The defence counsel then cross-examined him on the subject of insanity, forcing an admission from him that the borderline between sanity and insanity was often a very narrow one and that, if a man were predisposed to insanity, any great mental burden might easily push him over that borderline.

The counsel for the prosecution interjected that he had arranged for the doctor who had charge of Buckeridge while he was confined in Shrewsbury Gaol after the shootings to be present as a witness. Mr Justice Avory responded rather testily that, until the issue of the prisoner's mental condition was raised, it had nothing to do with the prosecution. There followed some legal arguments over the admissibility as evidence of a letter found in Buckeridge's possession after the shootings, which the judge decided to admit. Then, with the case for the prosecution concluded, the court adjourned for lunch, with the defence opening as soon as the proceedings resumed.

The first witness called by the defence was Buckeridge's mother, Mrs Sarah Buckeridge, who must have been very aware of the fact that her son's life may well be dependant on her testimony. Mr Milward gently led Mrs Buckeridge through her family history and the court learned that George's grandfather had 'a very queer state of mind' for the last four years of his life and was not safe to be left alone. In addition, one of George's aunts suffered from softening of the brain and had needed to be 'cared for' since she was a young child.

Asked about George, Mrs Buckeridge told the court that ever since childhood he had suffered from nerves, bad headaches and delusions. She related her son's Army service in France for most of 1917, saying that he was in hospital for some time afterwards, although she didn't specify why and Milward didn't press her for further details.

Mrs Buckeridge told the court that, while George was in the Army, his wife had lived both with her and with her own mother, Mrs Sainsbury. 'I could not call her a good wife,' Mrs Buckeridge stated, saying that Winifred had always maintained that she could not live with George as a wife but only as a housekeeper. After the break up of the marriage, George had been devastated and, according to his mother, was, at times, not really in his right mind.

Cross-examined by Mr Bosanquet, Mrs Buckeridge admitted that none of George's relatives had ever been in an asylum and neither had George. She also agreed that George, a bookbinder by profession, had always been in steady employment.

The defence called other witnesses to show how the break up of George's marriage had affected his life including a previous landlady, Mrs Agnes Pritchard, who told the court that George had been admitted to hospital for an operation in 1917 and had subsequently seemed very despondent and unhappy. He had eventually confided in Mrs Pritchard that his trouble was 'all through his wife', who had left him, and he feared that she would drive him mad. He was devoted to her, said Mrs Pritchard, and wanted nothing more than for his wife to come back to him. On one occasion, while Buckeridge was lodging with Mrs Pritchard, he received a letter from Winifred asking for money. Mrs Pritchard had been surprised that Buckeridge was still maintaining a home for his wife as well as sending her money but Buckeridge told her, 'There is nothing I would not do for my wife if I could only get her back again.'

Buckeridge sent money to his wife so frequently that he rarely had enough for himself, said Mrs Pritchard. Although he was far from well and suffering from frequent debilitating headaches, he tried to get an evening job to earn more money.

Another landlord, with whom Buckeridge lodged from the end of 1919 until May 1920, told the court that, at that time, his lodger's nerves were in a very bad state. Ernest Harris recalled that, on one occasion, Buckeridge had gone to visit his wife, returning with his face scratched and bleeding. An employer of Buckeridge's testified that he had suffered from nerves and headaches and that he had been dismissed from his work because the company feared that he was 'not in his right mind'.

The controversial letter found on Buckeridge on his arrest was then read out. It mainly dealt with Buckeridge's attempts to gain sufficient evidence of infidelity by his wife to divorce her, but finished with the curious phrase: 'I now shortly will be summing up that the girl is a washout and a ruiner of my life and the baby's, but the baby I shall save.'

The final witness for the defence was Dr John George Glynn, the medical officer from Shrewsbury Prison. Buckeridge had been sent there immediately after his arrest and had remained under Glynn's charge until 5 February, when Buckeridge was transferred to Gloucester Prison. During that time, Glynn had seen no signs of any insanity in Buckeridge.

The closing speeches by the prosecution and defence counsels were totally contradictory, with the prosecution insisting that Buckeridge was completely sane at the time of the shootings and the defence arguing otherwise. According to Mr Milward, Buckeridge was devoted to his wife and had never before shown any violence towards her. He had a familial predisposition to insanity and, on the day of the murders, something happened which was the accumulation of all that had previously occurred. 'The rush of the tide of the years of misery washed all the foundations of his sanity away,' concluded the defence counsel.

In his summary of the evidence for the jury, Mr Justice Avory reminded them that, in law, a man was presumed to be sane and responsible for his actions unless it was proved otherwise. Unless the question of Buckeridge's insanity had been proved to them without doubt, it was their duty to find him guilty of wilful murder.

This was exactly what the jury did. After an absence of thirty minutes, they returned to the court to pronounce Buckeridge 'Guilty' of the wilful murder of his wife, although they added a recommendation for mercy, given the circumstances preceding the shooting. Mr Justice Avory pronounced sentence of death on Buckeridge, promising to forward the jury's recommendation to the proper authorities.

The defence counsel announced their intention to challenge the sentence and the application to appeal was heard before the Lord Chief Justice, Mr Justice Sankey and Mr Justice Salter at the end of February 1923. It was the contention of Mr Milward that, in his summary for the jury, Mr Justice Avory had not given sufficient weight to the insanity defence. However, the Court of Criminal Appeal could find no criticism of Avory's summary and therefore refused Buckeridge leave to appeal his conviction.

Yet there is no record that George Vincent Buckeridge was ever hanged for his crime. The Criminal Lunatics Act of 1884 made it a requirement that any prisoner under sentence of death should be examined by two qualified medical practitioners if there was any suggestion that the prisoner might be insane, and it is reasonable to suppose that this was the case for Buckeridge. If so, his death sentence may well have been commuted to one of detention during His Majesty's pleasure.

Note: Most of the contemporary newspapers give the date of the Buckeridges' marriage as 1916. However, official records seem to indicate that it occurred in the last quarter of 1915.

21

'WHAT MADE ME DO IT?'

Pontshill, Weston under Penyard, 1924

The family at Croome Hall, Pontshill, gave every outward impression of living harmoniously. Thomas Blakesley Stevenson was a loving and affectionate husband and father to his wife Mary and his two sons. The youngest son, Alec, was in the Royal Flying Corps, while his older brother, Thomas junior, worked as a motor mechanic and still lived at home with his parents.

Thomas and Mary Stevenson had farmed 180 acres at Luscombe Farm at Snitterfield, near Stratford-on-Avon, until Thomas underwent an operation for appendicitis when the day-to-day management of the farm became too much for him and he decided to retire. The farm was sold and the family moved to Croome Hall. Thomas had mixed feelings about his retirement, on some occasions saying that he was glad to have given up farming and on others expressing regret at having sold the farm. Mary Stevenson had no such qualms – a keen gardener, she enjoyed pottering about in the garden and was delighted to shed the responsibility of the business and take things easy.

Although he had retired, Thomas Stevenson retained a keen interest in farming and, in August 1923, he and Thomas junior – usually known in the family as Ronnie – went on a three-month trip to Canada together as part of the Canadian Harvest Scheme. They spent their visit working on farms in Alberta and, according to Ronnie, his father seemed perfectly normal at the time, although he did suffer from a poisoned hand. It was only on his return to England that Stevenson began to appear depressed and, as the weeks passed, his condition grew gradually worse.

Stevenson was eventually persuaded to consult a doctor and Dr Dunlop of Ross-on-Wye found him to be severely depressed and suffering from chronic insomnia. Initially, Stevenson told Dunlop that he believed that his wife was not pleased to see

Pontshill. (© N. Sly)

Weston under Penyard, 1920. (Author's collection)

Weston under Penyard, 2009. (© N. Sly)

him back from Canada and, as his condition worsened, Stevenson came to believe that he was slowly being poisoned. Although he didn't accuse anyone outright, Dunlop formed the impression that Stevenson held Mary responsible and believed that she was not only doctoring his food and drink but also injecting things into his body in order to get her hands on his money.

Stevenson felt that 'people' were plotting against him and expressed a desire to 'shoot the lot of them'. Although his doctor prescribed treatment for him, Stevenson would never take any of the doctor's medication, preferring to treat himself with patent medicines and cure-alls that he saw advertised in the newspapers.

Dunlop eventually came to the conclusion that Thomas Stevenson was clinically insane and advised Mary that, for her own safety, she should have him certified and admitted to an asylum or private clinic for treatment. Mary Stevenson consulted with the family and returned to the doctor with the news that, although she and Ronnie agreed with his suggestion, her husband's brothers were very much against the idea.

Dunlop took it upon himself to call on one of Stevenson's brothers to try and convince him that it was in everybody's best interests for Thomas to be in a secure environment. The doctor told Henry Stevenson that he believed that his brother was certifiably insane and that, in view of his delusions that his wife was slowly poisoning him, Dunlop thought it highly probable that he would make an attempt to kill his wife if he were not treated urgently. Stevenson's brother could not be persuaded, insisting that his brother was harmless and refusing to allow the doctor to certify him.

Dunlop persisted and, on 3 March 1924, he finally persuaded Mary Stevenson to see sense. Dunlop filled in a lunacy certificate and got it countersigned by a second doctor, who had also recently examined Thomas Stevenson. He then arranged a bed for Stevenson at a private asylum, Barnwood House in Gloucester.

The certificate was handed to Mary Stevenson on 4 March and, on the following day, she called in to Dunlop's surgery to point out that he had made a slight mistake on the form. Dunlop corrected his error and Mary left, leaving Dunlop with the impression that she intended to have her husband removed from Croome Hall that afternoon. However, for reasons known only to herself, Mary Stevenson hesitated and her prevarication was to prove fatal.

Thomas Stevenson obviously learned of his wife's intentions, as his mental health deteriorated very rapidly after 5 March. On one occasion, his son found him in the washhouse, talking of fetching a rope from the garage and looking for a suitable place to hang himself. Ronnie immediately locked the rope away safely, confident that he had thwarted the latest of his father's threats to commit suicide.

By now, Thomas was almost completely unable to sleep and spent most nights wandering about the house, frequently going into his son's bedroom and asking to get into bed with him because he 'felt so ill'. To allow Mary to get some sleep, it was eventually decided that Thomas should move out of their marital bedroom and sleep in Ronnie's room, although he actually slept very little and, even when he did, was very restless and twitched and jerked constantly.

On 8 March, Thomas Stevenson called in at Ross-on-Wye police station and spent a couple of hours there writing a long letter, which he then handed to Superintendent J. Broad. The letter read:

To the Superintendent of Police, Ross on Wye. I, Thomas Blakesley Stevenson, wish to give myself up to the care of the police in consequence of the persecution and wrong treatment of my relatives and their employees. I complain that I have been or are about to be [sic] certified insane without sufficient reason and that I was under the influence of drugs given with criminal intent at the first examination and that, at the second one, I was said to be suffering from the delusion that I was being drugged, which was no delusion at all but true, as my condition now can prove. I complain that my relatives have employed medical men who have ruined my bodily health to fit me for the certificate of insanity and I believe I have two diseases now that I certainly did not have when they started doctoring me. I claim that I am not insane and certainly was not when medical men first took me in hand; and I claim that if I am insane now, it is through wrong treatment. Having reason to believe that criminal charges have been, or may be made against me, I make the above statement to claim the protection of the police or proper authority and ask that I may be placed in hospital and receive proper medical attention and thus given every chance to defend myself against any charges that may be brought against me.

The letter continued to accuse Mary Stevenson and other relatives of being involved in a 'cruel conspiracy' against the writer and begged for police protection against them.

Superintendent Broad had known Thomas Stevenson for about three or four months and believed him to be 'strange in his mind'. Broad set about convincing Stevenson that there was no criminal charge against him, a fact that Stevenson evidently struggled to comprehend. Finally persuaded, he returned to his home and to the family he was convinced were conspiring against him and trying to kill him. There he wrote similar letters and telegrams to the Chief Constable at Herefordshire, the Home Office and Scotland Yard, in which he claimed to be kept 'isolated and friendless' and implored them to intervene on his behalf, although there was no evidence to suggest that those letters were ever sent.

The morning of 15 March began much in the same way as every other morning at Croome Hall. The family ate breakfast, although Thomas was by now refusing to eat any food prepared for him by his wife and insisted on getting his own meals. Ronnie then went out to do some gardening. At eleven o'clock, he spoke to his mother, who told him that she was planning to go into Ross-on-Wye and was just going upstairs to put on her hat and coat. Although Ronnie didn't question his mother, he believed that the purpose of her visit to town was in some way to do with his father's illness.

Ronnie returned to his gardening and, just before lunch, his father came out to see him. 'I should like to plant a row of potatoes because it will be the last I shall ever plant,' Mr Stevenson remarked wistfully to his son.

Shortly afterwards, Ronnie went into the house for his midday meal. His father was in the kitchen at the time and watched him eating, although he wouldn't share his son's food. Ronnie then resumed his digging in the garden.

Less than an hour later, he was disturbed by a noise and looked up to see his father creeping stealthily towards him, holding a table knife in his hand at chest height, the blade pointing downwards. Ronnie waited until his father was close enough to touch him before grabbing his father's coat and spinning him around to face the house. His father didn't struggle, allowing his son to propel him forwards. It was only as they neared the kitchen door that Thomas suddenly said excitedly, 'I have done it. I have done it.'

'Done what?' asked Ronnie.

'I have killed your mother,' replied Thomas, who then lifted the knife to his own throat saying, 'Well, I will do for myself now.'

Ronnie snatched the knife from his father and ran to his motorcycle. Leaving his father in the garden, he rode to the police station at Ross-on-Wye, returning with PC Bowen and Dr Llewellyn B. Green. As soon as the three men entered the garden, Stevenson approached them and said to Bowen, 'Officer, I want to give myself up.' He then handed Bowen the key to the master bedroom door.

While Bowen waited outside with Stevenson and his son, Dr Green went inside and let himself into the bedroom. A bloody and torn mattress lay on the bedroom floor, with a woman's hat lying beside it. Green moved the mattress to one side and discovered the body of Mary Stevenson lying beneath it. Her face had been covered with a shawl, part of which had been thrust into her mouth. On the side of her head, between her right ear and temple, was a three-inch long wound, through which protruded pieces of brain matter and shards of bone. The wound appeared to have been made by a hard blow from an instrument with some kind of edge on it and had bled copiously. There was nothing in the bedroom that could have inflicted the wound but when Dr Green went back outside, he found a bloody hatchet in the washhouse.

Stevenson was driven to the police station at Ross-on-Wye, where his demeanour seemed strange and confused. He told Superintendent Broad, 'I am guilty, officer. What made me do it? Is she dead?' His brother, Henry, was called to see him and, when he spoke to Henry, it was evident that Stevenson had absolutely no recollection of what had happened earlier that day. Stevenson asked where Mary was and, when told that she was dead, argued that Mary and Ronnie were actually outside the police station in the car. When he was finally persuaded that this was not the case, Stevenson burst into tears and seemed inconsolable.

Although it was obvious that Stevenson was clinically insane, the magistrates at Ross-on-Wye still committed him for trial at the next Herefordshire Assizes. When his trial opened before Mr Justice Parfitt KC, Stevenson entered the dock wearing a black tie and sporting a black armband on his left arm, in mourning for his dead wife. He pleaded 'Not Guilty' to the charge against him.

The defence, conducted by Mr S.R. Bosanquet KC with Mr A.F. Clements, relied solely on proving that Thomas Blakesley Stevenson was insane at the time of the murder. As well as Dr Dunlop, they also called Dr M. Hampden Smith, the Medical Officer at Birmingham Prison, where Stevenson had been detained since 2 May, having been transferred there from Gloucester Prison.

Hampden Smith was asked if he had formed an opinion on the accused man's mental state, a question immediately objected to by the prosecution, who pointed out that the doctor was in court to relate facts not give opinions. Eventually, with the legal wrangling complete, Hampden Smith was allowed to state that he believed Stevenson did not know the nature and quality of his act and did not fully appreciate what he was doing when he struck his wife over the head with the hatchet.

The outcome of what even the counsel for the prosecution referred to as 'a very tragic and pathetic case' was inevitable. Thomas Blakesley Stevenson was found guilty but insane and ordered to be detained during His Majesty's pleasure.

22

'I FIRED AT HIM TO WOUND AND NOT TO KILL'

Sellack, near Ross-on-Wye, 1925

Fought during November and December 1917, the First World War Battle of Cambrai cost the lives of almost 44,000 British and 45,000 German soldiers, who were then fighting in France for their countries. Richard Louis Wreford-Brown, who served as a lieutenant in the 1st Battalion Welsh Guards, was one of the lucky ones who eventually returned to his home in Herefordshire. However, although he made it safely back from the front, he came back a broken man.

Wreford-Brown, who was described as a gentleman farmer in his civilian life, married Grace, the daughter of a Bristol doctor, in December 1918 and the couple went on to become the parents of two sons.

Yet Richard's health remained poor and he underwent three mastoid operations, leaving him with a suppurating wound that refused to heal. Invalided out of the Army following a gas attack, he was tormented by constant delusions. He came to believe that his wife was involved in a conspiracy against him and that she and others were tampering with his letters and drugging his food. By 1925, Richard's wife and mother were so concerned about the deterioration of his mental state that they visited his doctor, Dr Green, and asked him to see Richard on a professional basis. Green formed the opinion that his patient was suffering from stress and was in a very unstable condition mentally. He suggested to Richard's wife that she should send for her father, Dr Walter Carless Swayne.

Swayne, who lived in Clifton Park, Bristol, had always got on well with his son-in-law and willingly agreed to visit him at home to see if he could be of assistance.

Sellack. (© N. Sly)

The Ross from the Wye, 1950s. (Author's collection)

Swayne was a practicing physician, who was also professor of obstetrics at Bristol University.

The visit was arranged and on 13 August 1925, Wreford-Brown's mother went to collect Dr Swayne from Ross-on-Wye in her car and drove him back to her son and daughter-in-law's home, 'Sidonia', in the village of Sellack. Dr Swayne's son, Richard, was also visiting at the time and he spent the afternoon out on a car ride with his sister and brother-in-law. When they arrived home, the whole family spent a pleasant evening together.

Richard Swayne and his sister retired to their beds at just before eleven o'clock, leaving Richard Wreford-Brown downstairs in the smoke room talking to his father-in-law. Two hours later, Richard Swayne was abruptly awakened by the sound of gunshots and screaming.

The noise seemed to have come from the room next door to his bedroom – a room which his sister shared with her husband and her youngest son, who was still an infant and slept in a cot in the corner. Richard Swayne leaped out of bed and rushed across the landing to his sister's bedroom. Although the entire house was in darkness, there was sufficient light to enable him to see his brother-in-law silhouetted against the window, standing on an ottoman and wildly brandishing a revolver.

'The room is full of gas. They are trying to gas me,' screamed Richard Wreford-Brown, firing another two shots into the ceiling. Richard Swayne dropped to the floor and tried to wriggle across the room towards his brother-in-law on his stomach. When Wreford-Brown jumped off the ottoman and began to head towards him, Swayne scrambled to his feet again and ran off in search of some sort of weapon. Returning to his own room, he picked up the first thing that came to hand, which was a full jug of water and ran back to his sister's bedroom. However, Wreford-Brown was no longer there.

To his horror, Swayne realised that his brother-in-law was now in Dr Swayne's bedroom, still shouting hysterically about being gassed. Swayne heard his father calmly telling his brother-in-law that he was talking nonsense and should go back to bed but Wreford-Brown was beyond listening to advice.

'I am determined to get to the bottom of this,' he said firmly. 'Stand back a yard or I fire.' No sooner had he finished speaking than two gunshots rang out and Richard Swayne heard a loud thumping noise, as if something heavy had fallen to the floor.

Bravely, he rushed into his father's bedroom, which was in pitch darkness. He could just make out the figure of his brother-in-law in the blackness and managed to seize one of his arms with one hand, aiming a punch with the other arm at where he estimated his brother-in-law's body to be. The punch connected with some part of Richard Wreford-Brown, who immediately fell to the floor. Swayne climbed on top of him, grasped his throat with his left hand and groped blindly with his other hand, trying to locate the revolver. He was unable to find it, so remained on top of his brother-in-law, pinning him to the ground until his sister rushed into the room with two gentlemen named Napier, who were near neighbours. The Napiers managed to help to subdue Richard Wreford-Brown while the police and a doctor were called.

Richard Wreford-Brown soon quietened down and became docile and childlike as he was put to bed to await the arrival of the police. He seemed distraught at what had occurred earlier, asking constantly, 'What have I done?' and 'Have I hurt him?'.

Dr Green arrived at the house and tended first to Dr Swayne, who had been shot twice, once in the upper thigh and once in the stomach and was seriously wounded, although still conscious. Dr Swayne had been asleep in his bed when his son-in-law had burst into his room shouting. 'The second shot wasn't aimed. It was fired from the hip,' Dr Swayne told Dr Green. Green told Swayne that he had sent for a surgeon to attend to him but Swayne ruefully told him that it would be too late. He died from his injuries at about 9.45 that morning and the cause of his death was recorded as internal haemorrhage, resulting from the bullet wound to his abdomen.

While he was at Sidonia, Dr Green also examined Richard Wreford-Brown, who told him, 'I have been gassed. There was an attack on the house and I fired in self-defence.' When the police arrived, Wreford-Brown gave a similar account of his actions to Superintendent Broad, adding, 'The house is full of gas. They are trying to poison me. I told Dr Swayne to stand back a yard and he would not do so. I fired at him to wound and not to kill.'

An inquest was opened by Mr E.L. Wallis, the coroner for South Herefordshire, at which Richard Swayne was the chief witness, repeating his account of the events of the early hours of the morning of 14 August. Richard Wreford-Brown did not attend the inquest – having already appeared before magistrates charged with the murder of his father-in-law, he was now in custody at Gloucester Prison.

The coroner's jury recorded a verdict of wilful murder against Richard Wreford-Brown, adding a rider in which they requested that his state of mind should be inquired into when he stood trial.

By the time of his final hearing before magistrates at Harewood End Police Court, on 26 August, Richard Wreford-Brown had been judged insane and unfit to plead. Evidence was given by Dr Joseph D. Thomas, the superintendent of a private asylum near Bristol, who had examined Wreford-Brown at Gloucester Prison four days after the murder. Dr Thomas believed that the accused man was suffering from delusional insanity and that, when he shot his father-in-law, he had genuinely believed that he was defending his home and family in the face of a gas attack.

The medical officer at the prison agreed. Having observed Wreford-Brown over a period of several days, Dr James Bell had found him to be influenced by what Bell described as '... most definite, clear and persistent delusions.' Bell told the magistrates that, in his opinion, these delusions had been so pervasive that they had prevented Wreford-Brown from being able to distinguish between what was right and what was wrong, so that, at the time of the murder of his father-in-law, he could not appreciate the nature and quality of his actions.

The magistrates had no authority to take into account any evidence into the sanity or otherwise of the defendant and thus had no choice other than to commit Richard Wreford-Brown for trial at the next Hereford Assizes.

By the time his trial opened in November 1925, Richard Wreford-Brown's mental state had worsened. After pleading 'Not Guilty' to the murder, he began to shout from the dock:

> There has been a thing in Birmingham Prison. The marconigraph was put on me and
> I have been called different titles. I want the proof for those titles. One of the titles is
> Prince of Wales. I want that matter gone into. It alters the whole case.

After some calming words from the judge, Wreford-Brown was eventually persuaded to sit quietly, allowing Mr F.O. Langley to present the case for the prosecution.

Langley told the court that there was no evidence of any ill feeling between the defendant and his father-in-law. On the contrary, the two men had always been on the best of terms. Richard Swayne was called as a prosecution witness and, having repeated the evidence he had given at the inquest, he confirmed the excellent relationship between his father and brother-in-law, saying that the two men had always been very fond of each other. He continued to inform the court that Richard Wreford-Brown was a temperate man and that his brother-in-law's father had been an in-patient at an asylum for some time.

Dr Hamblin Smith, the medical officer at Winston Green Prison in Birmingham, to where Wreford-Brown had been transferred on 19 August, testified that, in his opinion, Wreford-Brown had been insane at the time of the murder and his condition had since deteriorated further, particularly over the past two weeks.

'He has been murdering me. That is why – murdering me the whole time,' shouted Wreford-Brown from the dock, struggling against the two warders who were trying to restrain him.

Given the mental state of the defendant, it was a foregone conclusion that the jury should find him 'Guilty but insane' and he was sentenced by the judge '... to be kept in custody as a lunatic until His Majesty's pleasure should be known.'

23

'I ASKED YOU NOT TO DO SUCH WICKED THINGS'

Burghill Court, near Hereford, 1926

Tuesday, 7 September 1926, started as an ordinary day for spinsters Elinor Drinkwater Woodhouse and her sister, Martha Gordon Woodhouse, aged sixty and fifty-seven-years-old respectively. After morning prayers, attended by all the staff, the sisters were served breakfast by their butler at their home Burghill Court, near Hereford. Yet shortly after finishing their meal, both sisters lay dead from shotgun wounds, Elinor shot through the head and Martha through the heart.

The two women had houseguests at the time – their cousin, schoolmaster Ernest William Jackson and his wife. At ten o'clock in the morning, Mr and Mrs Jackson were busy dealing with some correspondence in the room known as the smoke room, when they heard the unmistakeable sound of two gunshots. Mr Jackson locked his wife in the smoke room for her protection and ran downstairs. He found Elinor lying in a passage close to the kitchen and Martha slumped by the back door. Both women had obviously been shot and, while Elinor was clearly dead, Martha was still breathing, although terribly injured.

Ernest Jackson ran out of the house, shouting for the gardener and other servants. While someone was sent for a doctor and the police, every effort was made to render first aid to Martha. Sadly she died just as the police arrived at the house.

Conspicuous by his absence was the sisters' butler, forty-five-year-old Charles Houghton. Houghton had been in service to the Woodhouse family for twenty-two years, first as a footman, then as a butler. Once the police arrived, they began an immediate search of the house, finding the door of Houghton's room firmly locked.

Burghill Court. (© N. Sly).

Deputy Chief Constable Mr A. Weaver knocked on the door and demanded, 'Houghton, get up. Open the door.'

There was a sound from within the room and the door opened an inch or two before being slammed shut again. Weaver renewed his demands for the door to be opened and eventually Houghton emerged from the room onto the landing. He was bleeding from a number of wounds to his throat and thus Weaver's first priority was to get him to hospital to have his injuries attended to. As he led Houghton downstairs, Houghton reflected sadly, 'Oh, dear, this is a bad job,' adding, 'it was passion.'

The butler was taken to Hereford Hospital, where his wounds were cleaned and stitched. Meanwhile, the police had been interviewing the other staff at Burghill Court and had learned that, only the night before, the Misses Woodhouse had dismissed Houghton from his job for 'intemperate behaviour'.

According to the cook, Mrs Smith, Houghton had been fired because he had taken 'a little drop of something to drink'. His employers had believed that he had turned to alcohol over the previous summer and that his work had suffered as a result. When he accidentally dropped a dish of vegetables while serving dinner on 31 August, apparently under the influence of drink, his fate was sealed.

Since they were expecting Mr Jackson and his wife for a visit, the two sisters delayed sacking the butler until after their guests arrived, presumably feeling that they needed moral support and that the presence of another man in the otherwise all-female household would lend them the necessary authority to terminate Houghton's employment.

After more than twenty years in service to the same family, Houghton had been both angry and heartbroken to be ordered to leave the house within twenty-four hours, although he was given a month's wages in lieu of notice. Mrs Smith told the police that Houghton had protested that he needed more time and it was eventually reluctantly agreed that he would be permitted to stay for the rest of the week. Mrs Smith had tried to talk to the Woodhouse sisters on Houghton's behalf but Miss Elinor had dismissed her attempts to intervene, saying, 'I have seen enough during the last week and I must ask him to leave today.'

Mrs Smith also told the police that, immediately after the shootings, she had taken Houghton into the drawing room and asked him why he had done it. 'I do not know. I was mad,' he replied.

Houghton's wounds proved less serious than was first thought. He had made several half-hearted attempts to cut his own throat with a razor but the cuts were superficial and none were deep enough to be life threatening. Formally charged on his release from hospital with the murder of the Woodhouse sisters, his only comment was, 'I don't wish to say anything.'

An inquest was opened into the deaths of Miss Elinor and Miss Martha, at which the chief witnesses were Mr and Mrs Jackson and the family's cook, Mrs Smith.

Mrs Smith had obviously disagreed with Houghton's abrupt dismissal from his job, particularly as he had been so upset. She spoke of a conversation she had with him after the shootings in which she admonished him, saying, 'I asked you not to do such wicked things.'

'What did you mean by wicked things?' enquired the coroner.

Mrs Smith explained that Houghton had said that he would 'do himself in' after he lost his job.

'You did not hear him threaten to "do in" the Misses Woodhouse?' asked the coroner.

'No,' replied Mrs Smith.

Everyone who gave evidence at the inquest agreed that Houghton had seemed perfectly normal, if a little subdued, while he prepared and served breakfast on the morning of the murders. Then, having cleared away the breakfast dishes, he had gone to the pantry, where the double-barrelled shotgun was kept, loaded it and, in cold blood, shot both of his employers dead.

The gun belonged to Ernest Jackson and was used by him whenever he came to visit Burghill Court. The house stood on an estate of some 300 acres, which afforded excellent rough shooting. In such a small household, Houghton's duties were very light and he had been allowed to use the gun, often spending his mornings walking the grounds shooting.

Houghton appeared before magistrates at Hereford a week after the shootings, his throat bandaged. Committed for trial, Houghton stood before Mr Justice Swift

The grave of Elinor Drinkwater Woodhouse at Burghill. (© N. Sly)

The grave of Martha Gordon Woodhouse at Burghill. (© N. Sly)

at the next Hereford Assizes, on 5 November. Ronald Powell was counsel for the prosecution, while Houghton was defended by Mr A.J. Long.

The defence's assertion that the murder occurred while Houghton was having an epileptic fit did not sway the jury and they were quick to find Houghton 'Guilty' of the wilful murders of Elinor and Martha Woodhouse, leaving Mr Justice Swift to pass the mandatory death sentence.

Houghton was taken to the condemned cell at Gloucester Prison to await his fate. However, his original execution date was postponed when his defence counsel petitioned the Home Secretary with what they insisted was new evidence to support his defence claim relating to his epilepsy. However, all hope of a reprieve evaporated when the Home Secretary declined to interfere with Houghton's conviction and sentence. Houghton was hanged by Thomas Pierrepoint on 3 December 1926.

Note: In some contemporary accounts of the shootings, Martha Gordon Woodhouse is alternatively named May. Counsel for the prosecution is named as Mr Ronald Powell but, in other cases featured in this book, his forename is usually given as Rowland.

24

'SHAN'T I HAVE TO GO TO PRISON?'

At first glance, the death of thirty-one-year-old George Benjamin Parry seemed like a tragic suicide. Parry, who was unmarried and lived with his parents, was found sitting in a chair in the kitchen of Hunter's Hall at Lea, near Ross-on-Wye, a shotgun propped between his legs. Although he was said to be still alive when the police and a doctor were first called, by the time they arrived, Parry had died from what was apparently a self-inflicted gunshot wound to his neck and shoulder.

Parry, who was known to be a little 'simple', had been casually employed as a general manservant and handyman at Hunter's Hall for nearly nine years. He didn't live in but walked to work from his parents' cottage whenever he was needed.

On 9 January 1932, the only people present at Hunter's Hall were Parry and his employer, Mrs Edith May Dampier, a widow with two young children. Mrs Dampier called the police and, when they arrived at about 7 p.m., she told PC Matthews that she had been upstairs when she heard the sound of a gunshot from the kitchen. She rushed down to find Parry sitting mortally wounded in a high-backed armchair, her double-barrelled shotgun between his legs.

Mrs Dampier went on to tell PC Matthews that, earlier that day, Parry had been into the village and 'borrowed' two cartridges for the shotgun, saying that he wanted to shoot rats. Mrs Dampier had seen him in the kitchen, trying the cartridges to see if they fitted in the gun and had told him to put the gun down as he didn't understand how it worked. According to Mrs Dampier, Parry had argued that he knew what he was doing and that there was a 'safety thing' on the gun.

'Shan't I have to go to prison?' Mrs Dampier suddenly asked, under the mistaken impression that the mere fact that a man had died in her house would be enough for her to be incarcerated.

PC Matthews reassured her that she wouldn't but privately he was beginning to doubt Mrs Dampier's account of what had happened at the Hall that evening. He knew Mr Parry well and in view of his simplicity, would never have trusted him to handle a firearm. Parry was a kindly, inoffensive man who was always happy and, as far as the policeman was aware, had absolutely no reason to commit suicide. Yet if, as Mrs Dampier had stated, she had been alone in the house with Parry then there were only three possible explanations for Parry's death – either there had been an accident, he had killed himself or his employer had killed him.

When Dr John Dunlop arrived to examine the body, the latter explanation immediately seemed the most probable. For a start, the safety catch was engaged on the gun and it simply could not have been fired with the catch in the safe position. Dunlop noted that there was no blackening or singeing around the wound in Parry's neck, which he believed indicated that the gun had not been fired at close range but from some distance away. Although he said that it was not absolutely impossible for Parry's injuries to be self-inflicted, Dunlop was almost positive that someone else had pulled the trigger, as was Dr A. Greene from Ross who assisted with the post-mortem examination.

The police called on Home Office pathologist Sir Bernard Spilsbury and he too concluded that the cause of Parry's death was murder rather than suicide. Spilsbury believed that Parry could not have fired the shotgun from the position in which it was found – the trajectory of the shot showed that it had entered Parry's body horizontally and the only way in which he could have inflicted the type of wound that killed him was to have placed the shotgun on a table or similar, at some distance away, and pulled the trigger with the aid of a piece of string. Spilsbury's report stated that the shot had severed an artery in Parry's neck and also blasted away the top part of one of his lungs, causing his death from a combination of shock and loss of blood. The wound to Parry's neck would have killed him within a minute or so and,

Lea. (© N. Sly)

once shot, he would have been instantly paralysed from the neck downwards. Thus it would have been impossible for him to make any movement whatsoever. He could not have moved the shotgun, having fired the shot, and neither could he have moved the safety catch to the on position.

The police consulted with a London gun expert, Mr Robert Churchill, who concurred with Spilsbury's opinion. Having examined the gun, Churchill found it to be in perfect working order, although with a pull that was about one and a half pounds more than he would normally expect to find. Confirming that the gun could not be fired with the safety catch on, Churchill was then shown Parry's clothes and concluded that the gun had been fired from a distance of around 2ft away.

Of the three ways that George Parry could have died, accident was immediately ruled out as the shotgun's safety catch was on. Suicide was also eliminated, since the distance from which the gun had been fired was well outside Parry's reach. That left only one alternative – murder – and, since Mrs Dampier was the only other person present at the time of Parry's death, she was the only viable suspect. An inquest into Parry's death, held by coroner Mr C.B. Wallis, reached the same conclusion and Mrs Dampier was arrested.

'I didn't do it,' she insisted, after being arrested, charged and cautioned by Deputy Chief Constable Weaver.

Mrs Dampier was brought before magistrates, not at the usual magistrates' court but at a private hearing held at Ross-on-Wye police station. The only people present were two magistrates, Major R.W. Allen and Mr T. Richards, their clerk, the police officers, Mrs Dampier and her solicitor and a few representatives of the press. The sole purpose of the first hearing before the magistrates was to remand Mrs Dampier in custody pending a further appearance in the magistrates' court and it should have been nothing more than a formality. However, Mrs Dampier shocked everyone present by dramatically interrupting the proceedings.

'But I did do it. I did it accidentally,' she suddenly interjected.

Magistrate Major Allen immediately silenced her. 'Never mind that now. You need not say anything about it at present. You will come up on Friday next. Have you any objection to that?'

Mrs Dampier shook her head. The hearing was quickly brought to a close and she was taken to Cardiff Gaol to await her next appearance in court.

She was eventually to appear before magistrates a total of four times. It emerged that, on the night of the shooting, a baker, Mr Bradley, had been delivering bread in the area with his young assistant, Horace Hale. Hale had called at Hunter's Hall at between 5.30 p.m. and 6.30 p.m. and had been met by Mrs Dampier who had asked him to fetch Mr Bradley to the door. When Bradley got there, Mrs Dampier told him that George Parry had shot himself in the kitchen.

Bradley had baulked at going inside the house but had promised to fetch a neighbour. He called on Mr Onions, who lived nearby, but Onions was ill and could not go to Mrs Dampier's assistance. Hence Bradley went back and advised her to telephone for the police.

Having heard evidence from Sir Bernard Spilsbury and other medical witnesses, gunsmith Mr Churchill and Mrs Elizabeth Christopher, who had given the cartridges to Parry on the afternoon of his death, almost the last piece of evidence to be presented in court was that of Deputy Chief Constable Weaver, who related Mrs Dampier's admission at the private hearing. Mrs Dampier – who fainted during the proceedings and had to be revived by Sir Bernard Spilsbury – reserved her defence and, after a short consultation between them, the magistrates committed her for trial. She was sent to Birmingham Prison to await the start of the next Hereford Assizes.

Her trial opened before Mr Justice Roche on 12 February 1932, with Mr St John Micklethwait KC and Mr W.S. Morrison MP prosecuting and Mr Norman Birkett KC and Mr A.J. Long acting in defence of Mrs Dampier.

Although Mrs Dampier pleaded 'Not Guilty', it soon became evident that her defence team were not going to deny that she had committed the murder but were relying on being able to prove that she was insane at the time of the offence.

Dr Dunlop, who had been the first doctor at the scene of the murder, had also been Mrs Dampier's registered doctor and had attended her professionally for about five years.

Dunlop testified that he had been considering certifying Mrs Dampier insane before the murder. She had been tormented by the fact that she had transmitted a 'complaint' to her son, Robbie, which had caused him to lose the sight in one eye. She had frequently threatened to cut her son's eye out or to shoot the boy and then commit suicide. (Although it is not specifically mentioned by name, it seems most likely that the 'complaint' was syphilis, since it can be transmitted from mother to baby during childbirth, can cause blindness and, in its later stages, can lead to insanity.)

Although reluctant to discuss the exact nature of her illness in any detail, Dunlop was prepared to admit that he believed that Mrs Dampier had contracted her complaint from somebody who lived away from the area and that it had never occurred to him that she could have caught anything from Parry.

Another doctor who had treated Mrs Dampier, Dr H. Ward Smith from Hereford, also told the court of her bizarre behaviour prior to the murder. Ward Smith suggested that Edith Dampier had become obsessive, paranoid and delusional, convinced that people were pointing at her in the street and afraid to leave the house for long periods at a time because she believed that her appearance was attracting negative attention. Like Dunlop, Ward Smith had heard her threaten to commit suicide.

The defence then called two more medical witnesses. One, Dr G.W.T. Flemming, was the Superintendent of the Hereford County Hospital and had examined Mrs Dampier in Birmingham Prison on 4 February. It was Flemming's opinion that Mrs Dampier was definitely insane and had been so at the time of the murder, unable to understand the nature and quality of the act she was committing. Flemming told the court that Mrs Dampier purported to have seen her dead husband in person, even though he had been dead for many years and to have held long conversations with him since she had been in prison. For Flemming, that alone was sufficient evidence of insanity. Flemming's testimony was supported by Dr M. Hamblin Smith, the prison medical officer.

At the conclusion of the evidence, Mr Micklethwait declined the opportunity to address the jury on behalf of the prosecution, leaving the floor open for Mr Birkett to speak on behalf of Mrs Dampier. Birkett asked the jury to consider the accused woman's state of mind when arriving at their verdict, saying that on the dreadful day of the murder, there could not be the slightest doubt whatsoever that Mrs Dampier was insane in the truest and fullest sense of the word. Her actions on that night were inexplicable. Had Parry been someone who had done her some wrong then there would at least have been a motive but instead he had been a kindly, inoffensive man who had died purposelessly.

The defence counsel concluded his address by asking the jury to bring in a verdict of 'Guilty but insane'.

In his summary of the evidence for the jury, Mr Justice Roche told them that they should have no difficulty in coming to the conclusion that the correct verdict as far as the act of shooting the victim was concerned was 'Guilty'. However, the law stated that, if a person could satisfy the jury that he or she was insane, then there was legal provision for taking that insanity into account.

'What was at the bottom of it, no one will ever know, I suppose,' he continued, urging the jury to consider the folly of the act committed by Mrs Dampier, who had not murdered a person who had done her any harm but had instead killed an apparently innocent person. This fact alone may lead them to believe that she was, in ordinary parlance, mad. 'I do not think it is possible or probable in this case to contemplate any other verdict,' he concluded.

The jury were obviously in full agreement as they did not feel it necessary to retire and, after a brief consultation among themselves, which lasted for little more than a minute, pronounced Mrs Dampier guilty of the murder of George Benjamin Parry but insane. Mr Justice Roche ordered her to be detained during His Majesty's pleasure.

Note: In contemporary newspaper accounts of the murder, Parry's age is variously given as thirty-one and thirty-three years old. There is also some confusion regarding the identity of the first police officer to arrive on the scene. Initial reports name him as PC Moss whereas, in later accounts of the case, he is referred to as PC A.F. Matthews. It is not clear whether Moss and Matthews are two different police constables or whether Matthews was mistakenly called Moss in earlier accounts. The medical officer at Birmingham Prison is named Dr M. Hamblin Smith, although in other cases featured in this book, he is named Hampden Smith.

25

'I KNOW NOTHING AT ALL ABOUT IT'

Shobdon, 1935

On 19 July 1935, twenty-year-old Edith Agnes Nicholls left the cottage in Shobdon, where she lived with her parents, uncle and grandmother, to feed the family's chickens, which were kept in an adjoining orchard. Although Edie, as she was always known, was a very attractive young woman, she was rather studious and reserved. She was not known to have any boyfriends and, whenever she went out, she was normally accompanied by her mother.

It should have taken Edie no more than a few minutes to feed the hens and, when she hadn't returned after twenty-five minutes, her mother went out to the orchard to see what had happened to her. There Mrs Nicholls was faced with a sight that no mother should ever have to witness – the body of her daughter lying face down on the grass in a pool of blood. Mrs Nicholls dropped to her knees and lifted her daughter's head. Only then did she realise that it was almost severed from the young woman's body.

Mrs Nicholls let out a terrible scream, calling to her own mother, 'Mother, Edie has been murdered.' At the time, Walter Long, a travelling hawker, was tramping through the village with his wife and three children. He had just called at Mrs Elizabeth Powell's house, opposite Hillhampton Cottages where the Nicholls family lived, when he heard Mrs Nicholls' bloodcurdling shrieks.

Long immediately turned back to Mrs Powell's house, finding her on her doorstep trying to determine where the screams were coming from. 'There's something wrong at that house,' he told Mrs Powell before running across the road to see if he could be of assistance. He almost collided with Mrs Nicholls, who was rushing to ask Mrs Powell to summon a doctor. Mrs Powell ran to the village post office and

Shobdon, 1911. (Author's collection)

Shobdon, 2009. (© N. Sly)

asked postmistress Mrs Harris to call a doctor and the police, while Long went to Hillhampton Cottages to see if he could do anything to help. As soon he saw Edie, Long realised that nothing could be done to assist her and, having helped to cover the body, he went for the village policeman.

Soon there was a crowd of people gathered around the body in the orchard. Dr D.A.K. Cassels of Pembridge pronounced life extinct, after establishing that Edie's spinal column had been severed by blows from an axe or similar weapon. Looking around the orchard, he and Mrs Nicholls discovered a large, long-handled axe in some nettles, its head covered in fresh blood and brown hairs. Cassels pointed the axe out to the three police officers who were soon on the scene – PC David Morris from Shobdon, PC Harold Arrowsmith from Wigmore and Inspector Williams of Leominster, who were later joined by Deputy Chief Constable Superintendent G.T. Brierley from Hereford. By four o'clock that afternoon, the police had arrested a suspect who was taken to Wigmore police station and charged with wilful murder.

The suspect was Edie's uncle, twenty-seven-year-old Herbert Hughes, who lived with the Nicholls family at Hillhampton Cottages. At the time of the murder, Hughes had not been at home and, when police later found him leaning on the gate of the village cemetery at about ten past eleven, he told them that he had been for a walk to Mortimers Cross, leaving home immediately after eating his breakfast at eight o'clock. He denied having been anywhere near the orchard that morning and, when told that his niece had been murdered he expressed shock and surprise, saying, 'I know nothing at all about it.' However, PC Morris noticed that, while he was talking to him, Hughes continuously brushed his right trouser leg, which appeared wet. Asked why he was doing this, Hughes replied, 'To make myself look tidy.'

His suspicions aroused, Morris took Hughes to the police station at Wigmore, where his trousers were removed for closer scrutiny. When blood was found on the inside of one of the pockets, Hughes was cautioned and charged with Edie's murder. 'I know nothing at all about it,' he repeated.

A post-mortem examination conducted on Edie's body by Dr H.W. Johnstone, in the presence of Dr Cassels, showed that Edie had a total of six wounds on her body, all of which could have been made with the axe belonging to her father, which was found in the orchard immediately after her murder. There were wounds on her left forearm and right upper arm, suggesting that she had thrown up her arms to try and ward off blows from the axe, one of which had fractured a bone in her hand. There were three wounds on the back of Edie's neck, one on the left-hand side and two on the right, the largest of which was six inches long and three and a half inches deep. Finally, there was an oval-shaped wound on the left-hand side of her head that was roughly three inches long and two inches wide. Johnstone found no other signs of external violence and determined that the cause of Edie's death was a complete transverse fracture of her vertebral column. He confirmed that Edie had died a virgin and that her killer had not attempted to interfere with her sexually.

An inquest was opened into Edie's death by North Herefordshire coroner Mr H.J. Southall, at Leominster Cottage Hospital. Having dealt with evidence of identification and heard a report from Dr Johnstone, the coroner then adjourned the inquest and dismissed the witnesses.

Southall explained that there had been a recent change in the law, following the Armstrong case of 1921 (*see* chapter 19). If a coroner was informed that some person had been charged with the murder, manslaughter or infanticide of the deceased, before the jury had given their verdict, he should, in the absence of reason to the contrary, adjourn the inquest until after the conclusion of the criminal proceedings. In this case, Southall believed that he should exercise his full discretion in the matter and adjourn the inquest. It was not for the magistrates to decide guilt or innocence – all they had to say was whether or not there was sufficient evidence to commit the accused for trial – and Southall believed that the suspect in this case would most probably be sent for trial at the next Assizes. Thus he had no alternative but to wait for the result of the criminal proceedings although, if the occasion arose, he could always start the inquest afresh.

Stressing that his adjournment of the inquest would be in no way prejudicial towards the accused, Southall then formally discharged the jury, telling them that they would probably be very glad that they were not compelled to decide whether the accused was guilty or innocent of the most serious offence known to the law. Southall said that he did not personally know what the facts of the case were and he did not imagine that the jury wanted to know. Although relieved of their duties, the jury were still paid for their time and unanimously donated their fees to the British Red Cross Society.

As expected, the magistrates committed Herbert Hughes for trial for the wilful murder of his niece, granting him Legal Aid for his defence. The trial opened at Hereford on 2 November before Mr Justice Hawke, with Hughes pleading 'Not Guilty' to the charge against him.

The prosecution had discovered that Herbert Hughes was not a particularly welcome guest in his sister's home. Having moved into Hillhampton Cottages with his mother in January 1935, Hughes had recently been ill (although the exact nature of his illness wasn't specified) and had spent time as a patient in Hereford General Hospital and the hospital at Llandrindod Wells, returning to Shobdon on 13 July.

Hughes had always been very fond of his niece but had recently had a minor disagreement with her and taken offence at a remark she had made, which had sent him into a prolonged sulk. As a consequence, he had stopped speaking to Edie, after complaining that she wouldn't talk to him. The cause of the spat between uncle and niece was something so trivial that nobody could recall exactly what had triggered it but everybody agreed that Edie had not held a grudge against her uncle, had continued to treat him kindly and had not stopped speaking to him.

Plans and photographs of the orchard were produced in court and it was noted that there was one place where the boundary hedge was sparse enough for a person to be able to squeeze through it. However, the prosecution insisted that there had been no stranger in the orchard that morning and indeed, no strangers had been seen in the area at around the time of the murder.

Plenty of people had seen Herbert Hughes that morning, including hawker Walter Long, who was one of the first people on the scene when Edie's murder was discovered. Although Hughes and Walter Long had never met, the two men had engaged in a casual conversation having met on the road after Long had left the murder scene.

Hughes told Long that he had been for a walk and that he had left home at about eight o'clock that morning. He mentioned that he had eaten an egg for his breakfast but that he had not yet washed and told Long that his route that morning had taken him across the fields rather than into the village. Long asked if Hughes had seen him walking through the village earlier that day, telling him that he was with his wife and three children and that they had two prams with them. Hughes again denied being in the village that morning and, when he was arrested, gave exactly the same account of his movements to the police as he had already given to Long.

Yet Stanley Porter, a farm worker, gave a slightly different account. Walking along School Lane, he had heard running footsteps approaching him from behind, which came from the direction of Hillhampton Cottages. The running man – Herbert Hughes – caught up with Porter as he reached the stile at the end of School Lane.

Porter told the court that Hughes would normally have stopped for a chat but on that particular morning he seemed in a hurry. Porter wished him 'Good morning' and remarked that the grass needed cutting, but Hughes just answered 'Ummm' and carried on towards the post office.

George Wilson, the houseboy at Shobdon Rectory, had also seen Hughes that morning at about ten minutes to ten, when he was heading towards the cemetery. Wilson also wished Hughes 'Good morning' but Hughes did not reply and seemed to Wilson to be in a rush to get somewhere – or to get away from somewhere.

A third witness, Sidney Fletcher, had seen a man dressed in a dark grey suit near the War Memorial at Shobdon at about ten o'clock. Fletcher identified Hughes in court as the man he had seen and stated that his cap had been pulled down over his eyes as if he didn't want to be recognised and that he was walking very fast in the direction of Mortimers Cross. As Fletcher watched, the man quickened his pace even more.

Dr Johnstone gave evidence abut his findings at the post-mortem examination and the axe was produced in court. It was Johnstone's opinion that it would have taken considerable force to sever Edith Nicholls' spinal column, although he admitted that the blows could have been made by an average-sized woman. Asked whether Edie's murderer would have been covered in her blood, Johnstone told the court that he believed that the axe was too long and that the person wielding it would therefore have been out of range of any blood spilled in the course of the attack on the victim.

The only blood found on Herbert Hughes was some small smears on the inside of his trouser pocket. The trousers had been sent to Dr Roche Lynch, the Senior Official Analyst to the Home Office, who had determined that the blood was human in origin. However, Roche Lynch stated that even the slightest bleeding scratch or hangnail on Hughes' hand would have produced similar smears whenever he put his hand into his pocket.

Meanwhile, Hughes continued to insist, 'I know nothing at all about it.' He had never once wavered from his original account of his movements on the morning of the murder, saying that he had got up at eight o'clock, prepared himself an egg for breakfast then gone for a long walk, something that he was in the habit of doing.

In his summary of the evidence for the jury, Mr Justice Hawke told them that he could see no direct evidence to connect Hughes to the murder and that all the prosecution had was circumstantial evidence. The jury obviously agreed, since they returned a verdict of 'Not Guilty' and Hughes was discharged.

Edith Nicholls' grave at Shobdon cemetery. (© N. Sly)

Edith Nicholls' headstone. (© N. Sly)

On a research visit to Herefordshire, I spoke to several people who were children in the village at the time of the murder, all of whom had their own theories about what exactly happened on the morning of 19 July 1935. The most persistent of these theories was that, as she left the house to feed the hens, Edie put on a long, hooded cloak that belonged to her mother. Many people believed that whoever murdered Edie did so accidentally, having mistaken her for her mother, although nobody could think of any possible reason why Mrs Nicholls should have been the killer's intended target. Other people recalled that a man hung himself in the woods at Shobdon soon after the murder – some believed that it was Herbert Hughes, while others thought that it was Edie's grieving father, John Nicholls. Unfortunately, I have been unable to verify any of these recollections and hence I am not sure if they are factual or just legends that have gained momentum over the intervening years. So long after the murder, all it is possible to say with any certainty is that nobody was ever brought to justice for the brutal killing of Edith Agnes Nicholls.

Note: Edith Nicholls' age is variously given as twenty and twenty-one years old. PC Morris is also called PC Norris in some accounts of the tragedy and PC Arrowsmith's rank is sometimes given as Sergeant.

26

'WOULD IT BE RIGHT TO SAY YOU LOVED HIM DEARLY?'

Ledbury, 1947

It is not always pleasant to unfold such a story and it is not pleasant even for you, the jury, to look into the dark patches in the mind of a man whose mind may not be working and, indeed, could not be working in the same way as yours would work.

So said prosecuting counsel Eric Sachs KC, as he opened the murder trial held at the Hereford Assizes on 17 and 18 February 1948. It was a controversial trial that many people believed should never have taken place.

The victim was Cyril Ronald Barnes, aged twenty-three. Having been called up during the Second World War in September 1943, Barnes spent four and a half years serving in the Army in Italy and Austria before he was demobilised and returned to his home town of Ledbury. A trained motor mechanic, Barnes soon found a job at the Morgan Motor Company Ltd at Malvern Link and, on 9 August 1947, he married his girlfriend, Margaret.

In his spare time, Barnes was working on a motorcycle in a yard at the rear of Ivy House, near to his home in The Southend. For several years, Barnes had enjoyed a close friendship with a near neighbour, a forty-three-year-old piano tutor named Gilbert Charles Dundonald Griffiths. Griffiths had recently attended his friend's wedding and had played the organ at the ceremony but, once Barnes was married, the relationship between the two men seemed to change dramatically.

Four and a half years earlier, Griffiths had been absolutely distraught when his friend was called up. 'I will miss him more than my own mother,' Griffiths said

Ledbury, 1950s. (Author's collection)

tearfully and, when Barnes was posted abroad and the news of his posting was broken to Griffiths, according to Barnes' mother, Griffiths cried like a baby. While Barnes was away, Griffiths wrote to him telling him that he had been advised to make a will and that, if anything happened to him, Barnes was to receive £100.

The new Mrs Barnes often accompanied her husband when he went to repair the motorcycle and, whenever she did, Griffiths appeared very jealous. On one occasion he insulted her in her husband's presence, calling her a most objectionable name. He also once ordered the newlyweds to stop 'spooning' in his back yard. Both times, Barnes immediately packed up his tools and went home with his wife and gradually his visits to the yard became less and less frequent, almost as if he were distancing himself from his old friend.

On 15 October 1947, Barnes was working on his motorcycle when a shot suddenly rang out and he crumpled to the floor. He had been shot in the back and died from his injuries long before medical assistance could reach him. At a later post-mortem examination, carried out by Dr W.H. McMenemey of the Worcester Royal Infirmary, Barnes was found to have been shot from a distance of about 3ft. The discharge from the shotgun had entered his body forty-three inches above ground level, travelling in a slightly downwards direction and, according to the pathologist, would have caused Barnes to die within one or two minutes at most.

At a few minutes after midday, Gilbert Griffiths walked into the police station at Ledbury and approached the officer manning the desk, saying, 'Oh, Sergeant, I have shot my best friend.' Sergeant J. Bayley took a statement from Griffiths in which he persistently told the officer that he knew nothing whatsoever about guns. He told the sergeant that, having recently purchased the shotgun, he had taken it into the yard to show his friend. He had not loaded it and neither had he been aware that it was loaded. 'I must have touched the trigger, I suppose,' he said, sadly. However, when Bayley arrested him, Griffiths clammed up, now saying, 'I am not guilty and I have nothing to say at the moment.'

When Griffiths appeared before magistrates, they determined that there was a case to answer against him and committed him to trial at the next Hereford Assizes.

There, Mr Sachs, for the prosecution, tried to convince the jury that there had been 'an intimate liking' between the unmarried piano tutor and his young neighbour. Barnes' mother, Annie May Barnes, testified that her son and Griffiths had been 'on very friendly terms' since Cyril was fifteen years old and told the court about Griffiths' rather extreme overreaction when Cyril was called up to join the Army. The two men had often been for long walks together and Mrs Barnes admitted that, on one occasion, she had seen them walking with their arms around each others' waists. After Cyril's death, the letter from Griffiths concerning the bequest of £100 was found in his wallet.

Cyril's sister, Mrs K.J. Keeley, told the court that her brother had seemed somehow 'different' after his marriage. She also stated that, when Cyril married, Griffiths had said to her, 'I have nothing left to live for now.'

The prosecution then called witnesses to establish that Griffiths had bought both a shotgun and a pistol shortly before Barnes was killed. One of Griffiths' nephews, Mr K. Hall, told the court that he had asked his uncle to purchase a gun for him about eighteen months earlier, although he had been unaware that his uncle had actually bought a pistol. Mr Ronald Lewis of Ledbury sold the pistol to Griffiths two or three weeks before the murder.

Another nephew, Frederick Ellis, aged seventeen, testified to seeing a double-barrelled shotgun in two pieces at his uncle's home. Ellis had put the gun together and loaded it with one cartridge, having persuaded his uncle that it was a good idea to have it loaded for protection, since there had been a recent burglary near to his home and Griffiths had money in the house. It was also the height of the hop picking season, and the area was full of itinerant workers, some of whom had a well-deserved reputation for unlawful activities.

Ellis went on to say that, as soon as the shotgun was loaded, the safety catch automatically engaged. However, Ellis thought that his uncle was afraid of the gun and was confident that he wouldn't know enough about its workings to understand whether the safety catch was on or not. A few days before the murder, Ellis stated that he had asked his uncle if he might buy the gun from him and Griffiths had agreed to sell it to him for £9. Ellis was unable to raise the money and his uncle therefore kept the weapon with which Cyril Barnes was shot dead soon afterwards.

Yet, while most people agreed that Griffiths knew nothing about guns and seemed afraid of them, it was related in court that he had recently shown the pistol to Paul Hummell, a German prisoner of war from Ledbury Camp. Hummell and Griffiths met when Hummell expressed an interest in learning to play the piano and, when the German saw the gun, he was horrified to see that it was loaded and the safety catch was not deployed. When Hummell pointed this out, Griffiths told him that he hadn't been aware of this. Hummell showed him how to operate the pistol's safety catch and Griffiths made a note of his instructions in his notebook: 'Forward shoot, back safe.'

Counsel for the defence, Mr Long, reminded the jury that the onus of proof was on the prosecution. The whole case could be summed up in five words: 'Did Griffiths deliberately shoot Barnes?' and it was for the prosecution to prove beyond any possible doubt that Griffiths' actions on 15 July were deliberate, rather than a tragic accident.

Long called Gilbert Griffiths, who took the oath in a low, clear voice. Griffiths first discussed the nature of his relationship with Cyril Barnes, saying that he had known him since Barnes was about sixteen years old. Barnes loved music and, according to Griffiths, would often sit by an open window, listening to Griffiths playing the piano. Later, Barnes had sometimes helped Griffiths at concerts. According to Griffiths there had never been any 'words' between them, nor any misunderstandings.

'Would it be right to say you loved him dearly?' asked the counsel for the prosecution in cross-examination.

Griffiths answered this question by admitting that he 'thought a lot' of Barnes, having known him for a long time and that he had been very upset when Barnes was called up simply because he was fearful for his safety. The two men had what Griffiths described as 'a great affection for one another' but Griffiths insisted that he was glad when Cyril married Margaret because he knew that she would make him a good wife. He denied ever having sworn at Margaret or called her names and insisted that his remark about 'spooning' had been intended as a joke, even though Margaret had already testified that it had been said in an unpleasant way.

Mr Long then asked about the purchase of the shotgun and pistol. Griffiths said that he habitually kept money in the house – the police had found £270 in his wardrobe when they searched the house after the murder, although Griffiths maintained that there had been £362. There had been a recent burglary close to his home and he had bought the shotgun both for protection and because his nephew had asked him to buy one for him. He later bought the pistol because it was relatively cheap and he thought he could make a bit of money selling it on. He pointed out that the instructions written in his notebook referred to the pistol, which was not the weapon with which Cyril Barnes had been shot.

Griffiths admitted to lying to the police, telling them that the shotgun belonged to his father, but said that he had been afraid of being summoned for not having a licence and was also reluctant to implicate his nephew in the purchase of the gun.

'Did Mr Hall know that you knew nothing at all about guns?' asked Mr Sachs, adding that the defendant was hardly the most suitable person for Hall to ask to buy him a gun.

Griffiths was then asked about the will he had made, in which Barnes was named as a beneficiary of the sum of £100. Griffiths said that he had destroyed that will about seven or eight months after writing to Barnes and made a new will on 7 October in favour of his sister, Mabel.

Griffiths then gave his account of the events of 15 July. Barnes had been in the yard working on the motorbike and Griffiths had wandered over for a chat with him, asking him, 'Do you think you will get this bike to start quickly?'

'It will start off like a shotgun,' replied Barnes, reminding Griffiths that he had never shown his gun to his friend. He immediately went back into the house and fetched the gun from the attic to take it outside to show Barnes.

'I passed through the living room into the scullery and then the thing happened,' said Griffiths, continuing,

When I got to the scullery, I stepped down the steps but caught my heel on one and stumbled against the far end of the gas stove. This caused a sudden jerk forward of the gun and the 'spout' of the gun hit up against the door post.

Griffiths insisted that he had not consciously pulled the trigger and that he had no reason in the world for wanting to shoot his friend.

Unfortunately for Griffiths, a gun expert, Detective Inspector H.G.F. Bantock of the Birmingham City Police, had already testified. He had rigorously tested the gun to see if he could fire it accidentally, both by knocking it with his hands and by banging the stock against a wooden bench. Bantock had concluded that the trigger would need to be pulled before it could be fired. In addition, when the police took possession of the shotgun after the shooting, the safety catch had been engaged – would a man who purported to know nothing whatsoever about guns have done this?

The court was then told that Griffiths was not a well man. Dr C. Francis stated that the accused was suffering from a bone disease that caused him constant pain. In addition, he also had a chronic heart condition and, on 15 August 1947, Francis had informed him that his heart was 'an uncertain quantity'. Francis told the court that what he meant by that statement was that Griffiths was likely to die suddenly at any time.

It was pointed out in court that Griffiths had previously 'borne an exemplary character', one of the main character witnesses being Sergeant Bayley, who had known the accused since 1939. However, something seemed to have happened between Barnes and Griffiths on 7 October, when Barnes was seen by witnesses visiting Griffiths' home alone. On that date, Griffiths had written a letter to his sister, Mabel, which he left propped up on his mantelpiece. In the letter, Griffiths told Mabel that he was leaving her his money, wardrobe and piano and made no mention of any bequest to Cyril Barnes.

The two counsels then made their closing speeches. Mr Long spoke for three-quarters of an hour in defence of Griffiths, saying that his account of the events of 15 July could well be true and, if that were the case, then a verdict of wilful murder against his client would be 'a most unwarrantable conclusion.' Mr Long was followed by Mr Sachs, for the prosecution, who spent thirty minutes trying to persuade the jury that the accident theory was quite beyond belief. For the prosecution, the facts of the matter were quite straightforward – Griffiths' affections were centred on another man, rather than another woman. He advised the jury to try and consider the matter by thinking for a moment 'man equals woman', telling them that, while it was not a pleasant thought, it was exactly what had happened.

It was then left for Mr Justice Croom-Johnson to summarise the evidence for the jury. In a speech lasting for ninety minutes, Croom-Johnson first put before the jury an alternative verdict of 'manslaughter'. Saying that he did this with a certain amount of hesitation, Croom-Johnson pointed out that this would mean that they would have to find that there had been criminal negligence in Griffiths' handling of the gun, rather than any deliberate attempt to murder Barnes.

The prosecution was asking the jury to put two and two together on certain matters, continued Croom-Johnson, and many of these were 'trifles lighter than air.' For instance, there was no evidence whatsoever of any 'inordinate affection' between the two men. Had there been any 'unpleasant, perverted affection' between them, said the judge, then he felt sure that Barnes' mother would have had something to say about it. The prosecution had suggested that Griffiths had intended to commit suicide after killing Barnes, preferring to 'go with this dead soul into another world.' Croom-Johnson pointed out that there was not a shred of evidence to support this theory.

Finally, Croom-Johnson dealt with the motive for the killing. Motive, said the judge, was the most fallible of tests and, if the evidence they had heard in court convinced the jury that a murder had been committed, the motive for that murder was of no consequence.

With that, the court adjourned for lunch, after which the jury began their deliberations. The court resumed at 2.15 p.m., with the jury returning at 2.40 p.m. to pronounce the defendant 'Guilty' of the wilful murder of Cyril Ronald Barnes. Griffiths showed little reaction to the verdict and when asked if he had anything to say, he waited until the judge had put on the square of black silk to denote that he was about to pronounce sentence of death before saying in a shaky voice, 'I am not guilty.'

With Griffiths now on the verge of collapse, the judge pronounced the death sentence, struggling to conceal his own emotions as he did so and, at one stage, appearing to be on the verge of tears.

Griffiths was eventually reprieved by the Home Secretary in early March of 1948. Whether this reprieve was granted because of Griffiths' poor health, because of doubts about his sanity at the time of the murder or because of an inability to determine if the verdict should have been one of manslaughter rather than one of wilful murder is not known.

27

'THERE IS ALWAYS THE CHANCE THAT SOMETHING WILL HAPPEN'

Clehonger, 1952

At about 12.10 p.m. on 14 March 1952, Mrs Harris called at the Bungalow Stores in Clehonger to do some shopping. She found the shop door closed but unlocked and, on going inside, immediately noticed that the shop bell hadn't rung as it usually did to alert shopkeeper Maria Hill to the presence of a customer.

Looking around, Mrs Harris realised that the bell had come unscrewed from the door and she helpfully screwed it back on again. Still nobody came to serve her, so she went round to the back of the shop and checked the garage. Finding nobody there, she decided that Mrs Hill had probably popped out for a few moments and resolved to try again later.

Mrs Harris went back to the shop at 1.20 p.m. and, although she knocked and called out, there was still no response. At 2.10 p.m., when there was still no trace of Mrs Hill, Mrs Harris walked through the shop into the back room. There she found seventy-four-year-old Mrs Hill, lying on her side by the fireplace. Thinking that the elderly woman had collapsed, Mrs Harris rushed to help her but, on bending over the old lady, she quickly realised that Mrs Hill was beyond all help. Mrs Harris reported her discovery to a near neighbour, who telephoned for the police.

PC Allman arrived at about 2.30 p.m. and found Mrs Hill lying fully clothed on her living room floor, her slippers nearby. Although the ashes in the grate were cold, the elderly widow's head and face had been badly burned and, on closer examination, Allman noticed that she also appeared to have been stabbed. A woman's black jacket covered the lower half of her body but had evidently been placed over Mrs Hill's face after she had been attacked. There were scraps of charred paper and burnt rags scattered all around her body and it was later established that the paper had been torn from the current issue of the *Radio Times* and that the remainder of the magazine was missing.

Allman called in reinforcements and the Herefordshire Constabulary quickly sought the assistance of Scotland Yard. A post-mortem examination, carried out by Professor J.M. Webster, established that Mrs Hill had first been partially strangled by hand, which would have rendered her unconscious. She had then been 'hacked' seven times, five of the wounds being at the back of her head and the remaining two on her face. Finally, Mrs Hill's face and upper body had been badly burned, although it was unclear whether she had fallen unconscious onto the fire or whether the burned debris around her body indicated that her attacker(s) had attempted to set fire to the bungalow. Webster determined the cause of Mrs Hill's death to have been a combination of shock and loss of blood and stated that the burns to her head and face had occurred while she was still alive. He was of the opinion that she had died on the evening or night of 13 March and that her wounds had not been made with a knife but with a blunter, double-edged instrument, possibly a small chopping axe.

The police began house-to-house enquiries in the area and soon located Mr Preece, a steel fixer from the village, who had purchased some sweets at the shop at around 3.30 p.m. on 13 March. At that time, Mrs Hill was wearing a grey dress with a black jacket over it and had seemed perfectly normal. Initially it was thought that Mr Preece may have been the last person to see Mrs Hill alive but then Ann Smith came forward to state that she too had bought sweets from the shop that day at around 7.30 p.m. The shop door had been locked when Miss Smith had arrived but Mrs Hill had unlocked it to let her in and the two women had spent about fifteen minutes chatting before Miss Smith left to return home. While Ann Smith was there, Mrs Hill had brought an oil lamp into the shop from her living room and the lamp had still been burning at 10 p.m. that night, although it was not known whether or not Mrs Hill was alive at that time.

A native of Blaenavon in South Wales, she and her husband had originally moved to Herefordshire to keep a hotel in Pembridge. However, Mr Hill died soon after the couple took possession of their new business and Mrs Hill had promptly sold up and moved to Clehonger, purchasing the small bungalow that housed the shop, which she had run single-handed for almost twenty years. In spite of her age, she was an active lady, although according to those who knew her, she tended to 'keep herself to herself.' She was also very cautious, usually keeping the shop door locked, and did not admit strangers to the shop after dark, rarely allowing anyone at all into her private quarters. Thus it was theorised that either Mrs Hill had known her killer(s) or that the murderer(s) had entered the shop before darkness fell.

Mrs Hill had one son, Bonar George Hill, who worked at a social club in Malvern, travelling home to stay with his mother every weekend. On 14 March, he left Malvern at 8 p.m., arriving at Clehonger an hour later to find his mother's bungalow under police guard, with his mother lying dead inside. Bonar Hill was later taken to the mortuary at the County Hospital where he formally identified his mother's body.

He was able to tell police that the average takings from his mother's shop were around £7 a week, in addition to which Mrs Hill received her old-age pension. He confirmed that his mother had recently withdrawn £100 from her bank account and had paid the majority of the money into her savings account. He knew that she had kept about £30 back and that she usually kept her money in a wooden box in a wardrobe in the hall.

In all, Bonar Hill believed that about £60 had been stolen, although Detective Sergeant Davies of the Hereford CID had already found several small sums of money untouched in the house. The shop till still contained 12s 4½d and £1 14s 6d was found in a tea caddy. A bloodstained envelope contained a pass book for a West Midlands Bank savings account, into which were tucked three £1 notes, and an open, empty wooden box was found near the body, a bloodstain on the inside of its lid.

In addition to the £60, Bonar Hill told the police that his mother's accounts were missing. Mrs Hill had not kept formal accounts but instead had kept two small memo books. In one book she recorded the takings from the shop and in the other she noted any money that she spent. The police described the books as having red covers with black lettering, each book being roughly 4in x 3½in in size, and a public appeal was made through the newspapers for anyone who might have seen the books to come forward.

Also missing from the house were the remains of the *Radio Times* and Mrs Hill's pyjama trousers. The police were struck by the tidiness of the room which, apart from splashes of Mrs Hill's blood on the furniture, looked almost totally undisturbed. There were no signs that any struggle had taken place and whoever had robbed and murdered the old lady had not ransacked the premises. This supported their theory that Mrs Hill had known her attacker(s), who might have previously been invited into her living quarters, thus having the opportunity to familiarise themselves not only with the layout of the room but also with Mrs Hill's habits.

By 28 March, the police had interviewed more than 2,000 people in connection with Mrs Hill's death and followed up numerous lines of enquiry, all of which had led nowhere. The names and addresses of everyone who attended Mrs Hill's funeral were taken and everyone there was later interviewed. Army officers from the Royal Engineers were brought in to search surrounding gardens with mine detectors for the murder weapon, which was never found.

The bungalow was situated about 100 yards from a bus stop and police boarded buses and questioned all the passengers, asking them if they had noticed any strangers in the area or seen anyone getting onto or off the bus in the vicinity of the bungalow at around the time of the murder.

An appeal was made for drinkers at the Seven Stars Inn to come forward in the hope that one of them might have noticed something out of the ordinary on the night of 13 March. It was known that there was a light burning in Mrs Hill's house at 10 p.m., which coincided with the time at which the pub closed. Since the pub was less than half a mile away from the bungalow, the police were keen to talk to anyone who might have passed it on their way home.

A bloodstained coat was handed in to the police, who were quickly able to establish that it was not connected with the murder. Several anonymous letters and telephone calls were received, including one made to the officers of a newspaper, suggesting that, if the police were to search gardens in Eign Street, Hereford, they might find something to their advantage. Although the police visited Eign Street, nothing connected to the murder was discovered there and the police eventually dismissed the call as a hoax.

Various theories emerged about the identity of Mrs Hill's killer(s). One line of enquiry was that the killer could well have been a woman. Knowing Mrs Hill's reluctance to admit strangers into the shop, the police gave some weight to the suggestion that she may have made an exception for a woman. Having found no murder weapon, it was suggested that her wounds could have been made with a nail file or a pair of scissors, both of which were items that might routinely have been carried in a woman's handbag. Another theory was that the murder may have been committed by someone to whom Mrs Hill might have lent money, who may have been angered either by a refusal to lend a further sum or by a demand from Mrs Hill for repayment.

The police firmly believed that somebody, somewhere, knew the identity of Mrs Hill's killer(s) and was not coming forward either through fear or loyalty. The police appealed for that person to contact them, promising that he or she would receive full police protection and guaranteeing anonymity.

In spite of the exhaustive efforts of more than thirty officers, including two from Scotland Yard, when Mr C.W. Shawcross, the coroner for South Herefordshire finally closed the inquest into Mrs Hill's death on 22 May 1952, the police were no nearer to making an arrest and Shawcross recorded a verdict of 'murder by person or persons unknown'.

On 17 September 1952, an unusual report appeared in the *Manchester Guardian* stating that the police were following up a new line of enquiry. They had been contacted by a woman who had been a patient in the County Hospital, Hereford at the time of the murder. During the night of 13/14 March, the woman had experienced a nightmare so horrific that it had caused her to wake up the whole ward with her terrified screams.

When questioned by staff, the woman told them that, in her dream, she had witnessed an old woman being battered to death by a man in a place that looked like a house but was actually a small shop. So vivid was the dream that the woman was absolutely positive that she would recognise the man if she ever saw him again. The police interviewed the woman, along with the hospital staff and former patients but still no arrests were made.

In August 1955, when the investigation into the murder of Mrs Hill was more than three years old, one of the leading officers on the case, Detective Inspector R.J. Weaver, appeared as a guest speaker at the Ross-on-Wye Rotary Club. In the course of his talk, he intimated that the police knew who was responsible for Mrs Hill's murder but believed that they would never get enough evidence to make an arrest. Interviewed by newspapers on the following day, Weaver declined to elucidate further, simply saying, 'We are still making enquiries and police officers still visit the district. We pay particular attention to anyone who has been away from the village and returns after a period. There is always the chance that something will happen.'

Ironically, at the time of Maria Hill's death, only eight books were found in her house, all of which were murder mystery novels and, when she confronted her killer(s), Mrs Hill was apparently reading one of them with the aid of a magnifying glass. Unfortunately, unlike the cases featured in her favourite literature, there was to be no neat conclusion to the real-life murder mystery involving Mrs Hill herself.

28

'AN EYE FOR AN EYE, A TOOTH FOR A TOOTH AND A LIFE FOR A LIFE'

Leintwardine, 1968

On 18 November 1968, Dr Alan Avery William Beach of Leintwardine was holding his normal evening surgery. At about 7.15 p.m., Dr Beach was in the middle of a consultation with patient Dennis Holder when the telephone in his office rang. Whatever was said during the telephone call obviously led Beach to believe that he was urgently required to deal with a medical emergency, since he immediately closed his surgery for the night and left hurriedly, in spite of the fact that there were still several patients in the waiting room.

Soon afterwards, Terence Davis of Hopton Heath spotted a white car clumsily parked across the entrance to the driveway of a cottage. When Davis went to investigate, he found a severely injured man sitting in the driver's seat. The man had slumped sideways over the passenger seat and, although unresponsive, was groaning quietly. It was Dr Beach, who had terrible head wounds, having been shot with a shotgun, which had literally blown away a section of his head. Davis flagged down a passing car and the driver, Mrs Pandora Disley, stopped to see if she could help. Bending into the car to examine the badly wounded man, Mrs Disley immediately noticed a strong smell of whisky.

Dr Beach died very shortly after being discovered in the car, which was quickly connected to Arthur Frederick Prime, the proprietor of a hairdressing salon in Leintwardine. Prime had bought the three-litre Austin from a salesman on

15 November, even though he already owned a car. Although the official registration of the vehicle to its new owner had not yet been completed, PC David Pascoe, one of the police officers called to the scene, recognised it as identical to the one recently purchased by Prime and was also able to recognise a tan briefcase found in the vehicle as being very similar to one he had seen Prime using. The police appealed through the press for Prime to come forward to assist them with their enquiries.

Above & below: *Two views of Leintwardine. (Author's collection)*

On the following day, Dr Beach's car was found abandoned in a nearby field. Since there had been no response to the appeal for Prime to contact them, the police went to his home on Watling Street, Leintwardine. They arrived at about midday to find all the curtains at the house still drawn closed, although the inside of the windows appeared to be steamed up.

When the police could obtain no response from inside the house, Detective Chief Superintendent Robert Booth made a decision to force the door. Accompanied by two police dogs, Booth and another officer made a quick search downstairs before going upstairs to Prime's bedroom. There they found Prime lying in bed, deeply unconscious, a shotgun propped up by the side of the bed.

In the tension of the moment, Booth snatched up the shotgun and accidentally pulled the trigger, firing the gun and hitting his police dog. Even the sound of such a loud bang at close quarters didn't rouse Prime, who was completely comatose, apparently having taken an overdose of tablets. An ambulance rushed him to hospital, where he gradually recovered until, on 25 November, he was considered fit to be taken by ambulance to appear at a special sitting of the magistrates' court at Wigmore, charged with the wilful murder of Dr Beach.

There had been a history of disagreement between Prime and Beach stemming from the death of Prime's wife. Irene Prime had been a patient of Dr Beach's until she died suddenly in September 1967, at which time Prime had strongly believed that Dr Beach was responsible for her death. On 11 September, Dr Beach telephoned the then Leintwardine constable PC Jones. (Jones was subsequently promoted to Sergeant.)

As a result of that telephone conversation, Jones telephoned Prime, saying, 'I understand you have some trouble. Shall I come down?'

Prime agreed and when PC Jones arrived at his home, he found that Prime's wife had died. Dr Beach was apparently willing to certify Mrs Prime as dead but was refusing to issue a death certificate on the grounds that she had died very suddenly and he wanted a post-mortem examination conducted on her body to determine the actual cause of her demise.

PC Jones tried to persuade Prime to allow Beach to examine his wife's body but Prime, who was understandably distraught at the time, refused to allow Dr Beach to enter his home. 'I'm not letting him in,' he told Jones aggressively. Eventually Jones managed to convince Prime to permit Beach to certify the death of his wife but, once the doctor had left, Prime made a direct accusation to Jones that Beach had killed his wife. 'An eye for an eye, a tooth for a tooth and a life for a life,' Prime threatened ominously.

The post-mortem examination was held on Mrs Prime and her husband was further incensed by the fact that he wasn't allowed to attend the proceedings. He insisted that he wanted to be present to see what his wife died of and, when she was determined to have died from natural causes, he accused the doctors of being in league with one another and of closing ranks to protect one of their number. Told that he should contact the coroner for North Herefordshire if he had any concerns,

Prime replied that he intended to do so. 'This will ruin his practice,' he raged against Dr Beach, adding, 'I will make him pay for it.'

As the months passed, Arthur Prime seemed to be able to view the situation more rationally and his talk of vengeance against the doctor came to nothing. In due course, Prime even began courting Hazel Latimer, a shop assistant from Leintwardine and, in October of 1968, the couple became engaged, setting a provisional date of 4 December that year for their wedding.

In the meantime, Prime was experiencing problems in his hairdressing business. He had a falling-out with Miss Drury, a member of his staff, and consequently dismissed her from his employ. Unexpectedly, Miss Drury promptly announced her intention to set up her own salon, in direct competition with her former employer, a fact that infuriated Prime, who saw it as a slur on the memory of his wife and a deliberate attempt to destroy the business that she had worked so hard to build up.

Under extreme stress at the thought of Miss Drury opening a rival salon, at some point on or around 14 November 1968, Prime apparently made the fateful decision that his wife's death should be avenged. Thus, on the following day, he purchased a car for £1,435 and paid £47 10s for a 12 bore double-barrelled shotgun that was advertised for sale in the local newspaper, the *Hereford Times*. He then visited a shop in Castle Street, Ludlow, to buy cartridges for the gun, before sitting down to write a series of letters.

Having spoken to his fiancée by telephone, telling her that he would not be able to see her on 18 November as he had to go to a meeting in Wolverhampton, Prime subsequently wrote to her saying,

> I am not letting Miss Drury do her take-over. I'm sorry but my wife's memory is too vivid in my mind to let it happen. Thank you very much for your company. I've enjoyed it only I knew it could not last after last Thursday.

Prime's next letter was to his mother and included the words, 'I've had enough and can see no future in living any more. When Irene died, my world collapsed. I've tried to carry on but can't do so any more.'

His final letter was sent to the Hereford Constabulary, complaining that they had failed to take action on unspecified complaints that he had made to them. In this letter, Prime stated ominously:

> I've taken one or two decisions for you. I'm not of unsound mind. I'm not prepared to let you destroy my wife's business, which she slaved so hard to build up. I'm sorry for the scribble, only I am in a hurry to join my wife.

It was obvious from the tone of all three letters that Prime was contemplating committing suicide. However, it appears that he was also planning on killing Dr Beach first.

Arthur Frederick Prime was committed by magistrates to stand trial at the Hereford Assizes for the wilful murder of Dr Beach, a charge to which he pleaded 'Not Guilty' at the opening of proceedings in February 1969. Mr Justice Ashworth presided, with Mr C. Lawson QC and Mr R.B.C. Parnall prosecuting and Mr D. Draycott QC and Mr Northcote defending the accused.

The counsel for the prosecution opened the Crown's case by telling the jury that this was the clearest possible case of murder, which had been both carefully planned and premeditated. Dr Beach had died in a car purchased by Prime, from shots fired from a shotgun purchased by Prime, having been lured to his death from his surgery by a telephone call that Prime had made.

However, for the defence team, the evidence was not quite as conclusive as the prosecution would have the jury believe. When Mr Draycott took the stand, he spoke eloquently on behalf of his client, raising several points that seemed to cast doubts on what the prosecution undoubtedly regarded as a cut-and-dried case of premeditated murder.

Draycott told the jury that the prosecution had suggested that Prime had killed Dr Beach out of revenge because he was upset and distressed at what he saw as the medical mistreatment of his wife fourteen months earlier. Saying that it was perfectly normal for a man to be extremely distressed on the death of the wife he loved, Draycott pointed out that, in the fourteen months between Irene Prime's death and the murder of her doctor, Prime and Beach must have encountered each other several times, living as they both did in a relatively small village. Besides, four of the witnesses called by the prosecution had testified in court that Prime had not appeared to brood over his wife's death, neither had he seemed to hold a grudge against Dr Beach. One of those people had witnessed a discussion that Prime had engaged in shortly after Irene died, with somebody who wasn't aware of her death. That witness stated that Prime was then able to discuss his wife's death in a completely calm and rational manner. A second person had testified that she had never heard Prime try to blame anyone for his wife's death.

Prime had got over his wife's death to the extent that fourteen months later, he was preparing to marry again. His fiancée, Hazel Latimer, told the court that Prime had behaved perfectly normally throughout their entire courtship and had given no indications that he held Dr Beach in any way responsible for the death of his wife.

Draycott then addressed the letters that Prime had written shortly before he attempted suicide. The letters did not say 'I am going to murder a doctor and take my life after' said Draycott. On the contrary, they seemed to point to the fact that the dispute with Miss Drury over her rival business had been blown up completely out of proportion in Prime's mind until it had reached the stage where 'a molehill became a mountain'. These letters were clearly written by a man who was plainly unbalanced at the time of writing, stated Draycott. He then went on to examine the evidence, saying that there were several facts of the case that indicated that Prime was not the killer of Dr Beach.

Draycott first asked the jury to consider why Prime had bought the car when he already had a perfectly good vehicle of his own, particularly if he was contemplating suicide. 'What is the purpose of the car?' asked Draycott, answering his own question by pointing out that it had no point or purpose in the murder. A witness had seen Prime leaving his flat at 6.45 p.m. on the night of the murder, while she was drawing her curtains, and had clearly stated that, at that time, Prime was driving his old car. The purchase of the shotgun was insignificant, given that Prime was clearly intending to take his own life.

Although the prosecution had inferred that the telephone call made to Beach's surgery had been made by Prime, the call had been traced to a call box at Bedstone and connected by an operator, Douglas Ward, who was completely confident in his recollection that he had heard two voices from the call box, one male, one female. The call that lured Dr Beach to his death had clearly been made by two people, insisted Draycott, who then turned his attention to the scene of the crime.

Mrs Disley had testified to noticing a strong smell of whisky emanating from the car when she first opened the door. Blood tests conducted on both Prime and Dr Beach had shown that neither man had any trace of alcohol in his bloodstream. Besides, Mrs Beach had testified that, having known her husband for twenty-seven years, she had only ever seen him drink whisky about twelve times and then it was only one glass on special occasions. The strong smell of whisky indicated that someone other than Prime had been in the car at some point shortly before Mrs Disley had arrived.

Given the extent of Beach's head injuries, anyone who shot him should have been splattered with his blood. Tests on the clothes that Prime was wearing had discovered only one tiny spot of blood and that was on the inside of his trouser leg. There was nothing to suggest that it was Beach's blood – it could have been Prime's own blood or anybody else's and it could have been there for years.

Draycott then addressed a button found in the car, which was identical to those on Prime's jacket, which had a button missing. It was a common type of button, said Draycott, which could have come from Prime's clothing or from that of absolutely anybody else who had been in the car. It was not denied that Prime had purchased the car and he could easily have lost a button from his jacket at any time while he was in the vehicle in the three days between its purchase and the murder.

In fact, there had not been the slightest trace of physical evidence to connect Prime to the car. There had been no fingerprints found either on or in the vehicle and no fibres from his clothes. 'If he was driving that car, wouldn't there be evidence to connect him with it?' asked Draycott.

Numerous samples had been taken from the area around the scene of the crime and again, there was nothing to suggest that Prime had ever been there, with the exception of minute traces of soil on his shoes, which closely matched that from the scene of the killing. Even so, the tests could not show that the soil was limited to that particular area.

Mr Lawson then made his closing address to the court. Sergeant Jones' evidence that, at the time of his wife's death, Prime had been aggressive and threatening towards Dr Beach had not been challenged. What did the jury think that Prime meant by the phrase 'An eye for an eye, a tooth for a tooth and a life for a life', asked Lawson?

In spite of Prime's apparent outward normality at the time of the murder, it was obvious that something had reawakened his feelings for his dead wife and, at the same time, reawakened the feelings of anger, bitterness and vengeance for the man whom he blamed for her death. These were all the ingredients for the crime of killing the doctor, said Lawson, asking the jury why Prime should consider suicide at that particular time and intimating that it was a decision made to avoid the inevitable consequences of murder.

It was then left to Mr Justice Ashworth to sum up the evidence for the jury and his speech was twice interrupted by Prime shouting angrily from the dock in protest that he had not been allowed to give evidence. Ashworth pointed out that there had been no suggestion from the defence that the shotgun had been accidentally discharged. Neither had there been any attempt by the defence to demonstrate that Prime was temporarily insane at the time of the killing. In some cases, a plea of diminished responsibility could have been entered by the defence but, in this particular case, the defence was simply that Prime was not the man who shot Dr Beach.

'It most certainly was not,' interjected Prime at this point.

The judge continued as he had before, without acknowledging the latest interruption. He instructed the jury to apply their common sense and consider the case purely on the basis of the evidence submitted by the prosecution to determine whether they had proved beyond reasonable doubt that Prime was the murderer.

The jury took ninety minutes to consider the facts before returning a verdict of 'Guilty'. Addressing Prime, Ashworth told him that he had been convicted of this 'desperately brutal murder' on overwhelming evidence. 'The jury don't know but I and counsel do that your mental condition will require anxious consideration by doctors and I have no doubt that you will receive that consideration and any treatment when you are in prison,' Ashworth added, before sentencing fifty-one-year-old Prime to life imprisonment.

It is believed that Prime died in 1995.

BIBLIOGRAPHY & REFERENCES

NEWSPAPERS

Illustrated Police News
The Gloucester Journal
The Hereford Journal
The Hereford Times
The Manchester Guardian
The Times

BOOKS

Abbott, Geoffrey. *William Calcraft: Executioner Extra-Ordinaire*, Eric Dolby, Barming, 2004
Bruce, Alison. *Billington: Victorian Executioner*, The History Press, Stroud, 2009
Eddleston, John J. *The Encyclopaedia of Executions*, John Blake, London, 2004
Evans, Stewart P. *Executioner: The Chronicles of a Victorian Hangman*, Sutton Publishing, Stroud, 2006
Fielding, Steve. *The Hangman's Record Volume One 1868 – 1899*, Chancery House Press, Beckenham, Kent, 1994.

Various websites have also been consulted during the compilation of this book. However, since they have a tendency to disappear without notice, to avoid disappointment, they have not been individually listed.

INDEX